Creative Perspective

Susan Hunt

Creative Perspective

Robert W. Gill

with 176 illustrations

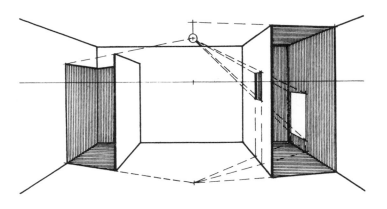

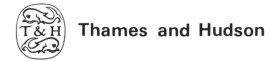

Thames and Hudson

Library of Congress Catalog card number 79–64609

Printed in Great Britain

Contents

1a Setting up a one-point perspective
view. Steps 1-7

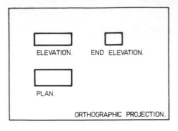

STEP 1. – OBTAIN INFORMATION.

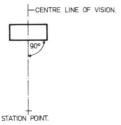

STEP 2. – LOCATE STATION POINT AND
THE CENTRE LINE OF VISION.

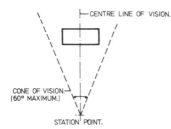

STEP 3. – CHECK. THE STATION POINT WITH
THE CONE OF VISION.

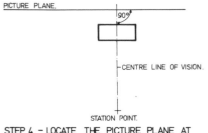

STEP 4. – LOCATE THE PICTURE PLANE AT
90° TO THE CENTRE LINE OF VISION.

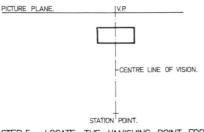

STEP 5. – LOCATE THE VANISHING POINT FOR
THE SIDES OF THE OBJECT PARALLEL TO
THE CENTRE LINE OF VISION . (SIGHT LINE.)

STEP 6. – LOCATE THE HORIZON LINE AND
PROJECT UP TO LOCATE THE VANISHING
POINT ON THE HORIZON LINE.

STEP 7. – LOCATE THE GROUND LINE.

Introduction

Before the basic principles of perspective projection can be developed and applied they must be understood. It is not intended here to become involved with the theory of perspective which has been fully explained in the companion volume to this one (see *Basic Perspective* by the same author). However, the methods for constructing a one-point, a two-point, and a three-point perspective are shown here to establish a starting point. The same basic principles are used in each of the three methods and it is only the relationship between the observer and the object which differs.

One-point perspective constructions (Fig. 1) are probably the simplest and quickest of the methods of setting up a perspective and are therefore popular with students. The eleven steps required to set up a one-point perspective view of an object are shown graphically and should need no further explanation. If the sequence shown is followed, little difficulty should be experienced in setting up any perspective view of this type.

In the case of a two-point perspective view of the same rectangular prism as used in Fig.1, twelve steps are required; these are shown in sequence in Fig. 2. Again, it is recommended that, to avoid unnecessary confusion, this sequence be followed when setting up a two-point perspective view of any object.

Fig. 3 shows the basic method for setting up a three-point perspective view of the rectangular prism used in the two preceding examples. Because the prism is tilted, i.e. its top and bottom are no longer parallel to the ground plane, a special plan is required before the perspective construction can be carried out. The method for preparing this special plan is shown in Fig. 3 together with the steps required, in sequence. The three-point perspective constructions are the most complicated of all the perspective constructions but when it is realized that they are only developments or extensions of inclined lines in perspective they should be more easily understood.

There are a number of variations of the basic method of setting up a three-point perspective view of an object. The third point,

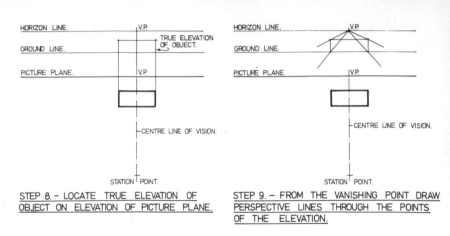

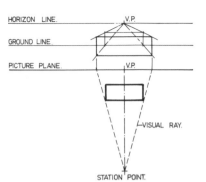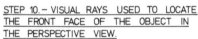

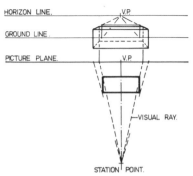

STEP 8. – LOCATE TRUE ELEVATION OF OBJECT ON ELEVATION OF PICTURE PLANE.

STEP 9. – FROM THE VANISHING POINT DRAW PERSPECTIVE LINES THROUGH THE POINTS OF THE ELEVATION.

STEP 10. – VISUAL RAYS USED TO LOCATE THE FRONT FACE OF THE OBJECT IN THE PERSPECTIVE VIEW.

STEP 11. – VISUAL RAYS USED TO LOCATE THE REAR FACE OF THE OBJECT IN THE PERSPECTIVE VIEW.

1*b*   Setting up a one-point perspective view. Steps 8-11.

which is the one which gives this method its name, is known as the vertical vanishing point, i.e. the vanishing point for those lines which were vertical in both the one-point and the two-point constructions. The example in Fig. 3 shows a three-point perspective based on a two-point construction. Three-point perspectives can also be based on one-point constructions and, though they are slightly simpler to construct, there is little difference in the underlying principles between them and the ones based on the two-point constructions. Another method which can be used to construct a three-point perspective view of an object is the one which uses an inclined picture

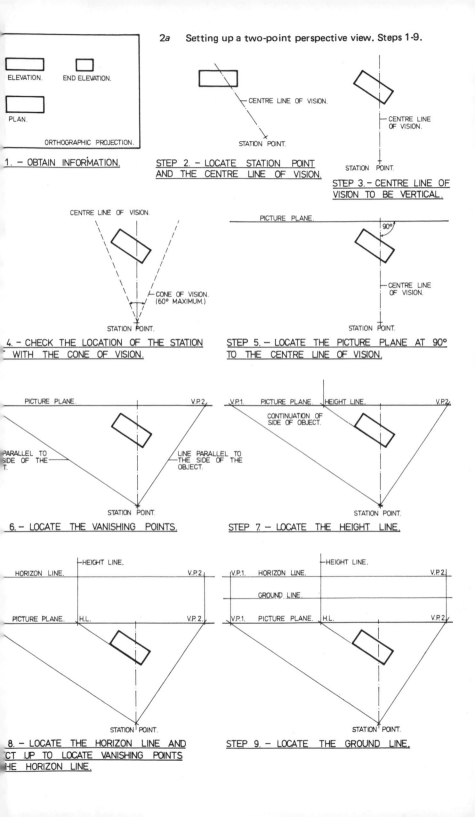

2a Setting up a two-point perspective view. Steps 1-9.

ELEVATION. END ELEVATION.

PLAN.

ORTHOGRAPHIC PROJECTION.

1. – OBTAIN INFORMATION.

CENTRE LINE OF VISION.

STATION POINT.

STEP 2. – LOCATE STATION POINT AND THE CENTRE LINE OF VISION.

CENTRE LINE OF VISION.

STATION POINT.

STEP 3. – CENTRE LINE OF VISION TO BE VERTICAL.

CENTRE LINE OF VISION.

CONE OF VISION. (60° MAXIMUM.)

STATION POINT.

4. – CHECK THE LOCATION OF THE STATION WITH THE CONE OF VISION.

PICTURE PLANE.

90°

CENTRE LINE OF VISION.

STATION POINT.

STEP 5. – LOCATE THE PICTURE PLANE AT 90° TO THE CENTRE LINE OF VISION.

PICTURE PLANE. V.P.2.

PARALLEL TO SIDE OF THE T.

LINE PARALLEL TO THE SIDE OF THE OBJECT.

STATION POINT.

6. – LOCATE THE VANISHING POINTS.

V.P.1. PICTURE PLANE. HEIGHT LINE. V.P.2.

CONTINUATION OF SIDE OF OBJECT.

STATION POINT.

STEP 7. – LOCATE THE HEIGHT LINE.

HEIGHT LINE.

HORIZON LINE. V.P.2.

PICTURE PLANE. H.L. V.P.2.

STATION POINT.

8. – LOCATE THE HORIZON LINE AND CT UP TO LOCATE VANISHING POINTS HE HORIZON LINE.

HEIGHT LINE.

V.P.1. HORIZON LINE. V.P.2.

GROUND LINE.

V.P.1. PICTURE PLANE. H.L. V.P.2.

STATION POINT.

STEP 9. – LOCATE THE GROUND LINE.

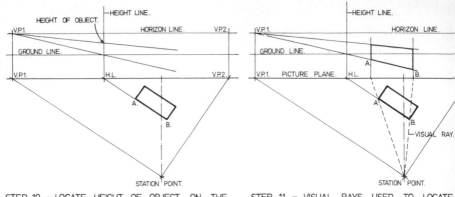

STEP 10. — LOCATE HEIGHT OF OBJECT ON THE HEIGHT LINE AND THE TOP AND BOTTOM LINES OF SIDE A - B IN THE PERSPECTIVE VIEW.

STEP 11. — VISUAL RAYS USED TO LOCATE POINTS 'A' AND 'B' IN THE PERSPECTIVE VIEW OF THE OBJECT.

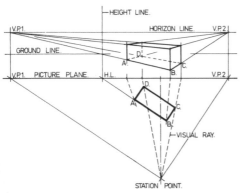

STEP 12. — VISUAL RAYS AND PERSPECTIVE LINES TO COMPLETE THE PERSPECTIVE VIEW OF THE OBJECT.

2b Setting up a two-point perspective view. Steps 10-12.

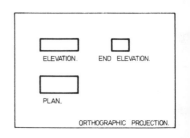

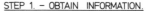

STEP 1. — OBTAIN INFORMATION.

3 Setting up a three-point perspective view. Steps 1-11.

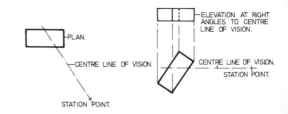

STEP 2. — LOCATE STATION POINT AND CENTRE LINE OF VISION.

STEP 3. — PREPARE AN ELEVATION AT RIGHT ANGLES TO THE CENTRE LINE OF VISION.

LOCATION OF SPECIAL PLAN
AND PLAN CONSTRUCTION.

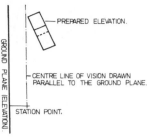

GROUND PLANE (ELEVATION).

PREPARED ELEVATION.

CENTRE LINE OF VISION DRAWN
PARALLEL TO THE GROUND PLANE.

STATION POINT.

STEP 4. – LOCATE AN END ELEVATION OF THE GROUND PLANE
AT RIGHT ANGLES TO A NORMAL PICTURE PLANE. LOCATE
STATION POINT, EYE-LEVEL, CENTRE LINE OF VISION AND
THE PREPARED ELEVATION IN ITS REQUIRED POSITION.

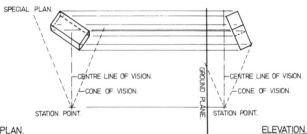

SPECIAL PLAN.

CENTRE LINE OF VISION.
CONE OF VISION.
STATION POINT.

GROUND PLANE

CENTRE LINE OF VISION.
CONE OF VISION.
STATION POINT.

PLAN.   ELEVATION.

STEP 5. – LOCATE PLAN OF THE CENTRE LINE OF VISION
IN A CONVENIENT POSITION — BY HORIZONTAL PROJECTION
AND MEASUREMENT THE SPECIAL PLAN IS PRODUCED.
(CHECK LOCATION OF STATION POINT WITH THE CONE OF VISION.)

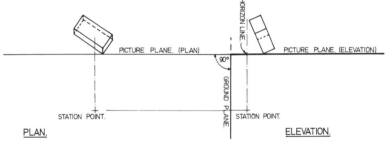

PICTURE PLANE. (PLAN)

HORIZON LINE.

PICTURE PLANE. (ELEVATION)

90°

GROUND PLANE

STATION POINT.   STATION POINT.

PLAN.   ELEVATION.

STEP 6. – LOCATE THE PICTURE PLANE (IN BOTH THE
PLAN AND THE ELEVATION) IN A CONVENIENT POSITION.

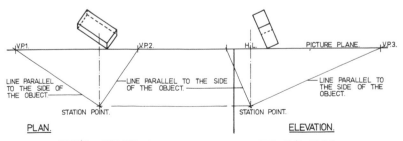

V.P.1.   V.P.2.   H.L.   PICTURE PLANE.   V.P.3.

LINE PARALLEL
TO THE SIDE OF
THE OBJECT.

LINE PARALLEL TO THE SIDE
OF THE OBJECT.

LINE PARALLEL TO
THE SIDE OF THE
OBJECT.

STATION POINT.   STATION POINT.

PLAN.   ELEVATION.

STEP 7. – LOCATE VANISHING POINTS IN BOTH THE PLAN
AND THE ELEVATION.

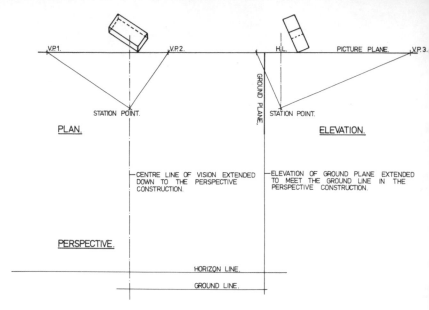

PLAN.

ELEVATION.

PERSPECTIVE.

CENTRE LINE OF VISION EXTENDED DOWN TO THE PERSPECTIVE CONSTRUCTION.

ELEVATION OF GROUND PLANE EXTENDED TO MEET THE GROUND LINE IN THE PERSPECTIVE CONSTRUCTION.

HORIZON LINE.

GROUND LINE.

STEP 8. – LOCATE THE HORIZON LINE AND THE GROUND LINE IN A CONVENIENT POSITION EITHER ABOVE OR BELOW THE PLAN. EXTEND THE GROUND PLANE TO MEET THE GROUND · LINE IN THE PERSPECTIVE CONSTRUCTION AND ALSO EXTEND THE PLAN OF THE CENTRE LINE OF VISION DOWN.

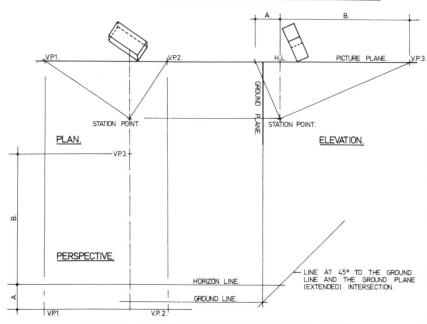

PLAN.

ELEVATION.

PERSPECTIVE.

HORIZON LINE.

GROUND LINE.

LINE AT 45° TO THE GROUND LINE AND THE GROUND PLANE (EXTENDED) INTERSECTION.

STEP 9. – MEASURE HEIGHTS OF V.P.3. (B) AND V.P.4. (A) ABOVE AND BELOW THE HORIZON LINE IN THE ELEVATION. LOCATE V.P.3. AT HEIGHT 'B' ABOVE HORIZON LINE AND V.P.1. AND V.P.2. AT HEIGHT 'A' BELOW IT. DRAW A LINE AT 45° TO THE INTERSECTION OF THE GROUND LINE AND THE GROUND PLANE.

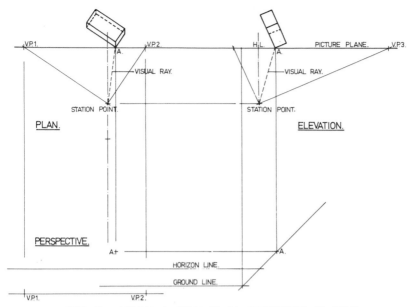

STEP 10. – LOCATE A POINT 'A' IN PERSPECTIVE BY USING
A VISUAL RAY TO LOCATE THE POINT ON THE PICTURE
PLANE AND THEN USING PROJECTIONS.

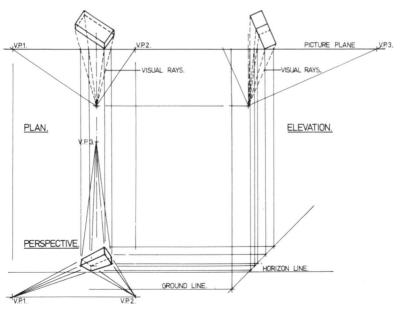

STEP 11. – USING VISUAL RAYS, VERTICAL AND HORIZONTAL
PROJECTIONS AND PERSPECTIVE LINES THE PERSPECTIVE
VIEW OF THE OBJECT IS COMPLETED.

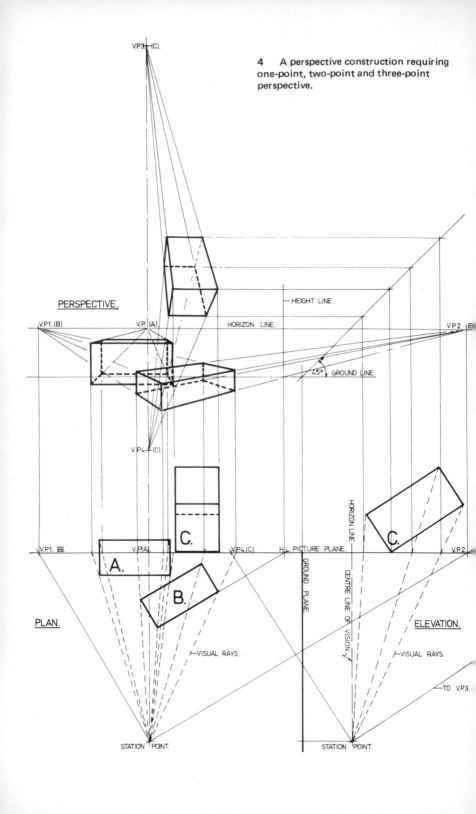

4   A perspective construction requiring
one-point, two-point and three-point
perspective.

plane. This method has an advantage over the one shown in Fig. 3 in that it does not require a special plan: this makes it eminently suitable for such large-scale aerial perspectives as city developments, airports etc. If an inclined picture plane is used for this type of subject a normal orthographic plan, such as the ones used in one-point and two-point constructions, can be used.

If the methods shown and discussed here are examined it will be seen that the basic principles are the same in each case, which means that they can be combined in the same drawing if required. Fig. 4 shows a composite drawing in which a one-point, a two-point and a three-point construction are used to portray the three different objects as they would be seen by an observer located at the station point. Once it is clearly understood that the basic principles of perspective projection do not change because the position of an object being viewed changes in its relationship to the observer, it is possible to go on to the next step. This step is the development, expansion and application of these basic principles so that they can be used to produce accurate perspective drawings with a minimum amount of wasted time and effort.

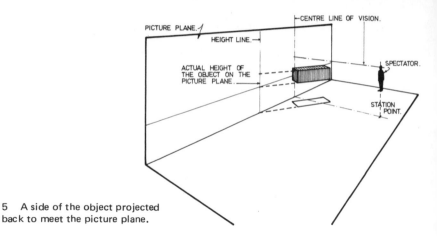

PICTURE PLANE.

CENTRE LINE OF VISION.

HEIGHT LINE.

ACTUAL HEIGHT OF
THE OBJECT ON THE
PICTURE PLANE.

SPECTATOR.

STATION
POINT.

5   A side of the object projected
back to meet the picture plane.

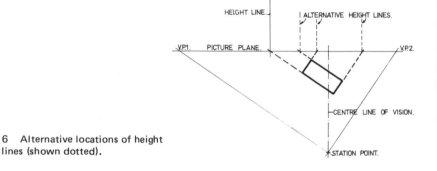

HEIGHT LINE.

ALTERNATIVE HEIGHT LINES.

V.P1.   PICTURE PLANE.

V.P.2.

CENTRE LINE OF VISION.

STATION POINT.

6   Alternative locations of height
lines (shown dotted).

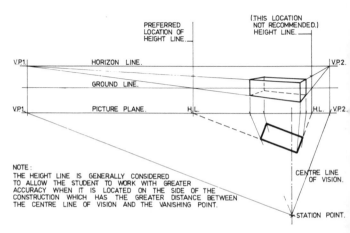

PREFERRED
LOCATION OF
HEIGHT LINE.

(THIS LOCATION
NOT RECOMMENDED.)
HEIGHT LINE.

V.P1.   HORIZON LINE.   V.P2.

GROUND LINE.

V.P1.   PICTURE PLANE.   H.L.   H.L.   V.P2.

NOTE:
THE HEIGHT LINE IS GENERALLY CONSIDERED
TO ALLOW THE STUDENT TO WORK WITH GREATER
ACCURACY WHEN IT IS LOCATED ON THE SIDE OF THE
CONSTRUCTION WHICH HAS THE GREATER DISTANCE BETWEEN
THE CENTRE LINE OF VISION AND THE VANISHING POINT.

CENTRE LINE
OF VISION.

STATION POINT.

7   Preferred location for the height
line.

1 The use of alternative height lines for more complicated shapes

The height line in perspective drawing is the line used for measuring all vertical heights relating to the object being drawn. These heights are measured using the same scale as that used for the preparation of the plan and elevations of the object being used in the perspective projection. The location of this line is found by projecting a convenient side of the object (in plan) either backwards or forwards as necessary to meet the plan of the picture plane. From this point a vertical line is drawn on the elevation of the picture plane and it is on this line that vertical heights can be measured. Fig. 5 shows graphically the relationship between the plan and the actual side of the object projected back to meet the picture plane. From this it can be seen that the top and bottom of the extended side meet the picture plane on the line projected up from the plan location of the height line and because the top and bottom lines of the object are parallel the distance between them remains the same when they are projected to meet the height line. Therefore heights can be measured on the height line because it is in fact a continuation of the side being measured.

Any side of the object can be projected either forwards or backwards as necessary to locate a height line. Fig. 6 shows each of the four sides of the object projected to meet the picture plane, resulting in four alternative locations for the height line. Each location will be accurate because each height line is located by projecting a side of the object back to meet the picture plane. However, the most convenient height line is the one usually accepted. In this case it is the one which was located by projecting the side of the object used to locate the vanishing point which is the further from the centre line of vision (V.P.1. in this case). The use of this height line rather than one of the alternative ones is considered to result in more accurate work because when the angle between two intersecting lines is small it is more difficult to locate the point of intersection than when the angle between the lines is nearer to a right angle. This can be understood by reference to Fig. 7 which shows a perspective line passing through a point measured on a height line at a small angle,

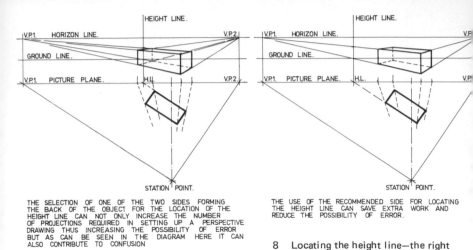

THE SELECTION OF ONE OF THE TWO SIDES FORMING THE BACK OF THE OBJECT FOR THE LOCATION OF THE HEIGHT LINE CAN NOT ONLY INCREASE THE NUMBER OF PROJECTIONS REQUIRED IN SETTING UP A PERSPECTIVE DRAWING THUS INCREASING THE POSSIBILITY OF ERROR BUT AS CAN BE SEEN IN THE DIAGRAM HERE IT CAN ALSO CONTRIBUTE TO CONFUSION

THE USE OF THE RECOMMENDED SIDE FOR LOCATING THE HEIGHT LINE CAN SAVE EXTRA WORK AND REDUCE THE POSSIBILITY OF ERROR.

8 Locating the height line—the right and the wrong way.

i.e. from a vanishing point close to the centre line of vision, and one passing through a point on a height line at a much greater angle, i.e. from a vanishing point at a much greater distance from the centre line of vision.

The reason one of the two unseen sides of a simple rectangular object is not normally used to obtain the height line, though either could be used, is simply a matter of convenience. If one of these two sides were chosen it would require at least one extra set of projections which could consume extra time and increase the chance of error. Fig. 8 shows the extra set of projections required when one of the unseen sides is chosen for locating the height line and, for comparison, the use of the recommended side to obtain the height line which eliminates the extra set of projections.

Once the use of the height line is understood in its simplest form it can be used to save a great deal of time in the setting up of perspective drawings of more complex objects, and objects consisting of a number of components. Figures 9a, 9b and 9c show three methods used to set up two simple rectangular prisms of different heights. It could be done using one height line but this would involve a large number of projections, as shown in Fig. 9a, which illustrates the method using a side of the lower prism to locate the height line. The projections required to draw the higher prism are unnecessarily complicated if this side is chosen. In this example there are two other alternatives open to the student. A separate height line can be used for each of the objects as shown in Fig. 9b. However, if the objects are examined it will be seen that only one height line is needed

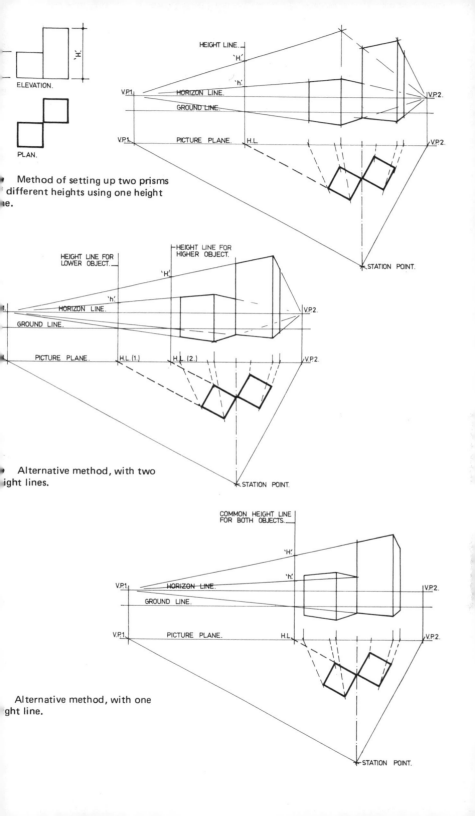

ELEVATION.

PLAN.

Method of setting up two prisms different heights using one height line.

HEIGHT LINE.
'H'
'h'
V.P.1. HORIZON LINE. V.P.2.
GROUND LINE.
V.P.1. PICTURE PLANE. H.L V.P.2.
STATION POINT.

HEIGHT LINE FOR LOWER OBJECT.
HEIGHT LINE FOR HIGHER OBJECT.
'H'
'h'
HORIZON LINE. V.P.2.
GROUND LINE.
PICTURE PLANE. H.L. (1.) H.L. (2.) V.P.2.
STATION POINT.

Alternative method, with two height lines.

COMMON HEIGHT LINE FOR BOTH OBJECTS.
'H'
'h'
V.P.1. HORIZON LINE. V.P.2.
GROUND LINE.
V.P.1. PICTURE PLANE. H.L V.P.2.
STATION POINT.

Alternative method, with one height line.

because if a side of the taller prism is projected back as shown in Fig. 9c, it coincides with a side of the shorter prism. In this case the use of this common height line will simplify the work required in setting up these two objects in perspective and not reduce the degree of accuracy, which is very important.

When confronted with a more complex shape in perspective drawing, such as the one shown in Fig. 10, it is often impossible to locate a common height line and therefore each part of the object must be treated as a separate object and a separate height line must be located for each part. In this case the first part to be drawn is the lowest section; this simplifies the drawing of the part located on it and the medium-height part can be left until last.

When preparing a perspective drawing of an object it is important to examine all of the possibilities so that unnecessary work is either eliminated or kept to a minimum, because unnecessary work often

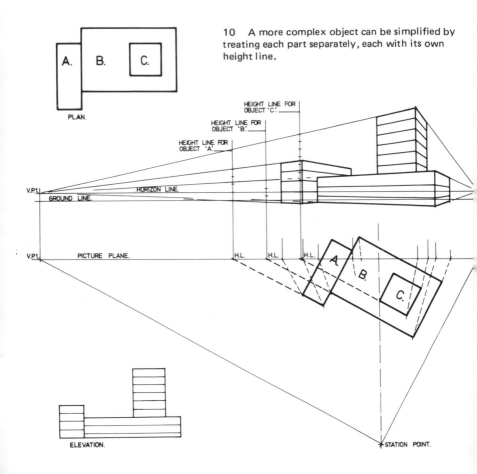

10   A more complex object can be simplified by treating each part separately, each with its own height line.

leads to the possibility of errors as well as wasted time. Fig. 11 shows a commonly encountered problem which can be greatly simplified if a second height line is used. In this case the pitched roof should be considered first and a height line for the roof located. The pitched roof should be treated as if it were a simple object containing inclined lines. When the roof is completed the walls of the building can be considered as a separate object, for which a separate height line will be required. This approach minimizes the amount of work necessary to produce a perspective drawing of an object of this type.

Once the delineator realizes that he is not limited to one or in fact any given number of height lines when drawing a perspective view of an object he will find that the use of alternative height lines is a great time-saver; if he exploits each one fully, he will avoid many inaccuracies which may otherwise occur in his work.

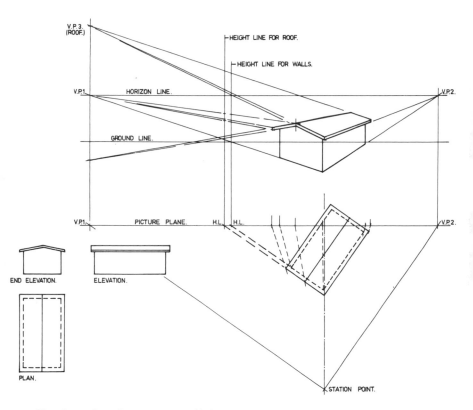

11 A case for using two separate height lines.

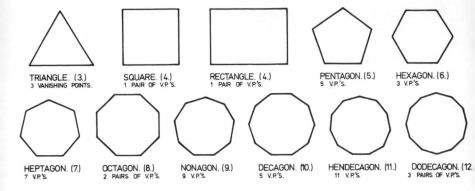

TRIANGLE. (3.)
3 VANISHING POINTS.

SQUARE. (4.)
1 PAIR OF V.P.'S.

RECTANGLE. (4.)
1 PAIR OF V.P.'S.

PENTAGON. (5.)
5 V.P.'S.

HEXAGON. (6.)
3 V.P.'S.

HEPTAGON. (7.)
7 V.P.'S.

OCTAGON. (8.)
2 PAIRS OF V.P.'S.

NONAGON. (9.)
9 V.P.'S.

DECAGON. (10.)
5 V.P.'S.

HENDECAGON. (11.)
11 V.P.'S.

DODECAGON. (12
3 PAIRS OF V.P.'S.

12   Eleven regular shapes, and the number of
vanishing points required in each case, for setting
up the shape in perspective.

13   The basic method of drawing a hexagonal
object, using three vanishing points.

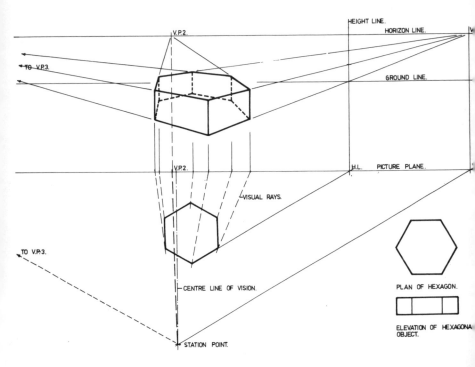

2 Regular and irregular shapes

Regular shapes, which include squares, rectangles, triangles, and regular polygons, create no special problems. Drawing squares and rectangles in perspective has been covered thoroughly in *Basic Perspective* so it is not intended to consider them further here. However, such shapes as triangles, pentagons, hexagons, heptagons, octagons, etc. are sometimes encountered in perspective drawing and the student should learn to examine the shape to ascertain firstly whether any of its sides are at right-angles to another side and secondly whether any of its opposite sides are parallel to each other. These two factors dictate the number of vanishing points required to draw any of these shapes in perspective. For example, a hexagon is a six-sided figure in which no side is at right-angles to any other side but which consists of three pairs of parallel sides: therefore only three vanishing points are required to draw a hexagon in perspective. If a triangle and a pentagon are examined in the same way it will be seen that the triangle will also require three vanishing points, and the pentagon will require five (Fig. 12). Pairs of vanishing points are required when a shape has sides at right-angles to other sides, e.g. a square, a rectangle, an octagon, etc. The reason for this should be readily understood by referring to the basic principles of perspective projection. Fig. 13 shows the method used for setting up a perspective view of a simple hexagonal object. The selection of a station point, the centre line of vision and the location of the picture plane are the same as for any other shape. The location of the horizon line and the ground line is exactly the same as for any other perspective drawing of an object situated on the ground plane. The height line is located by projecting any convenient side back to the picture plane in the usual way and, similarly, each of the vanishing points is located by drawing a sight line from the station point parallel to the side to be drawn to meet the picture plane. If this is done in sequence, so that each side is drawn in the perspective view before the next is considered, drawing a hexagonal shape is no more difficult than drawing a simple rectangle.

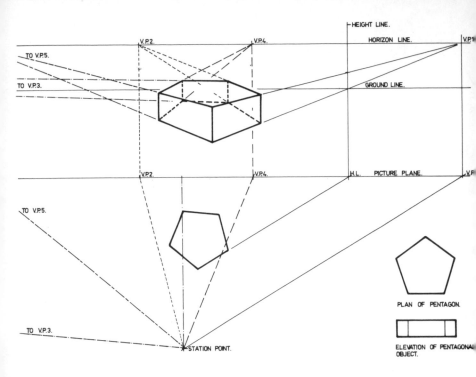

14 The basic method of drawing a pentagonal object, using five vanishing points.

A pentagon, unlike the hexagon, does not have any of its sides parallel which means that each side requires its own vanishing point (Fig. 14). Therefore five vanishing points will be required to draw it in perspective. None of its sides is at right-angles to any other side, therefore pairs of vanishing points will not be required. The method is the same as for the hexagonal object except that five vanishing points are required instead of three. Some shapes, such as a triangle, pentagon or hexagon, can sometimes be drawn in perspective by simpler methods. The most popular of these is to construct a square around the shape, as shown in Figs. 15 and 16, because when the shape is contained in a square it can be drawn in simple two-point perspective by locating on the square the points where the shape contained in it touches the sides of the square. This method of setting up an object in perspective is known as 'placing the object in a box', and by this method even the most

24

TRIANGLE. (3.)   PENTAGON. (5.)   HEPTAGON. (7.)   NONAGON. (9.)   HENDECAGON. (11.)

15   Five regular shapes 'in the box' (with squares constructed around them to allow perspective drawings to be made using a one-point or two-point construction). Where some of the points of the object do not touch the sides of the square, as in the heptagon, the nonagon and the hendecagon, lines are drawn from the centre of the object through these points to intersect the sides of the square. These points of intersection on the sides of the square can be used in the perspective construction in much the same way as the actual points of the object which do touch the sides of the square.

16   An alternative method of setting up a perspective view of a pentagonal object, using a square constructed round the plan of the object and simple two-point projection.

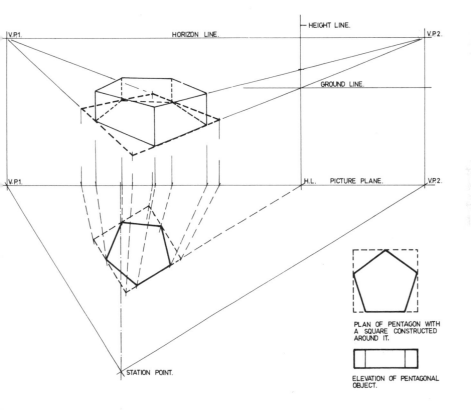

PLAN OF PENTAGON WITH A SQUARE CONSTRUCTED AROUND IT.

ELEVATION OF PENTAGONAL OBJECT.

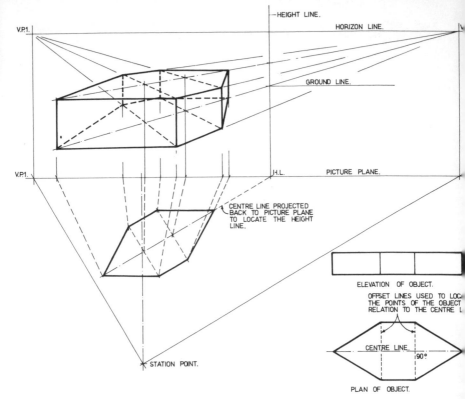

HEIGHT LINE.

HORIZON LINE.

V.P1.

GROUND LINE.

V.P1.   H.L.   PICTURE PLANE.

CENTRE LINE PROJECTED
BACK TO PICTURE PLANE
TO LOCATE THE HEIGHT
LINE.

ELEVATION OF OBJECT.

OFFSET LINES USED TO LOC
THE POINTS OF THE OBJECT
RELATION TO THE CENTRE L

CENTRE LINE.   90°

STATION POINT.

PLAN OF OBJECT.

17   The use of a base line (which in this example
is also the centre line) and offsets to set up a perspective drawing.

complex shapes can be drawn in simple one-point or two-point perspective. This 'box' method of drawing objects is dealt with more
fully in Chapter 4 (pp. 33-34).

Another method which can be used in special cases for drawing
regular shapes in perspective involves the use of a centre line at
right-angles to one of the sides. This side and the centre line can
be set up as a simple one-point or two-point perspective and the
other points of the shape can be located by using offsets from the
centre line. This is the usual method for irregular shapes but it can
be applied in some cases to regular-shaped objects with considerable
success.

When dealing with irregular shapes such as irregular quadrilaterals,
irregular polygons or irregular curves the use of a base line which can
be established to suit the shape, together with offsets to locate the
changes of direction, makes even the most complex shapes compara-

26

tively easy to draw in perspective. A simple shape such as the one shown in Fig. 17 can be set up in two-point perspective by drawing a centre line of the object on the plan together with two offsets on each side of the centre line (which is used as the base line in this example). The offsets are always drawn at right-angles to the base line, which means that the base line and the offsets, instead of the sides of the object, are used to locate the height line and the vanishing points. Once these are established, the rest of the set-up is exactly the same as for any other two-point perspective.

The construction shown in Fig. 17 is for an object which is symmetrical about a centre line but from this example it should be clear to the student that this method will work equally well for an object which is not symmetrical about a centre line. The irregular multi-sided object shown in Fig. 18 does not have a centre line about which it is symmetrical so a convenient base line must be established, together with sufficient offsets to locate all of the points where the sides of the object change direction. (It should always be remembered that the offsets must be at right-angles to the base line.) Once the base line and the offsets are established, this object can be drawn in simple one-point or, as here, two-point perspective. This

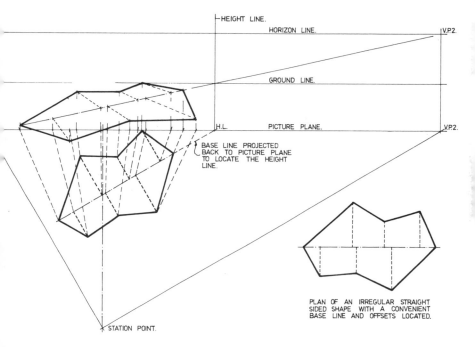

PLAN OF AN IRREGULAR STRAIGHT SIDED SHAPE WITH A CONVENIENT BASE LINE AND OFFSETS LOCATED.

18   For an asymmetrical object, a base line is arbitrarily drawn as convenient, with offsets to the outside angles of the object.

method is not limited to shapes with straight sides but can be used with considerable accuracy for irregularly-shaped objects whose sides are made up of constantly changing curves, such as the example shown in Fig. 19. In this case the greater the number of offsets used the greater will be the accuracy of the perspective drawing of the object.

There are no hard-and-fast rules for locating the base line for an irregularly-shaped object; the student should use his judgment and locate the base line in the position which eliminates as much unnecessary work as possible.

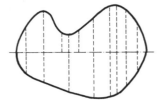

19 An irregular curved shape with a convenient base line and offsets located. The more offsets used, the greater the accuracy of the resulting perspective drawing.

3 Perspective drawings with a grid over the plan

When none of the above methods seems to give the complete answer to a problem involving complex shapes an alternative which can be used is the grid method. Fig. 20 shows part of a map, somewhat simplified for the purpose of illustrating the method of setting up a perspective drawing of an object of this type. With particularly complex shapes such as this the use of a base line and offsets is not always advisable. Instead a simple grid can be constructed over the whole of the part of the map or object forming the subject of the perspective drawing thus producing a series of simple squares which can be drawn quickly and easily in either one-point or two-point perspective.

A grid of suitable size should be adopted with regard to the character and scale of the object to be drawn in perspective (Fig. 21). Fig. 22 shows the method of setting up the grid in two-point perspective and locating the outline of the map by using visual rays through the points in the plan where the outline of the map intersects the lines of the grid superimposed on it. In this way an accurate perspective drawing of this part of the map can be obtained. If, in addition, the contour heights are available, it is possible to obtain not only the correct outline in perspective but also the accurate rise and fall of the land. The result is a complete and accurate picture of this part of the map in perspective. From the example in Fig. 23 it should be obvious that the height of the land above each intersection of the grid can be found. These heights (calculated from some base level, such as sea level in the example here) can be measured on the height line and projected in the normal way to their appropriate intersection, thus locating the level of the land at that point. This may be a tedious and time-consuming task but it has a number of applications, particularly where large building projects covering large areas of land are involved, or other developments such as bridges or large landscaping projects where accuracy is demanded in a basic perspective drawing.

The use of a grid over a complex shape has many other uses in perspective drawing besides the one shown here. By using a grid a complicated mural or a free-form pool together with many other objects of

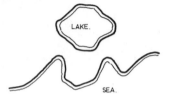

20 Part of a simplified map, to be drawn in perspective.

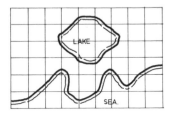

21 Grid superimposed on Fig. 20 to simplify the drawing of the map in perspective. Any convenient size of grid can be chosen, depending on the accuracy and the amount of detail required.

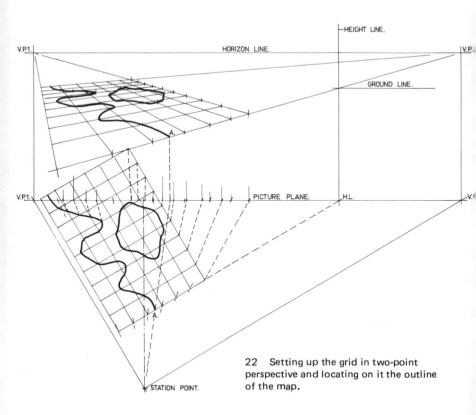

22 Setting up the grid in two-point perspective and locating on it the outline of the map.

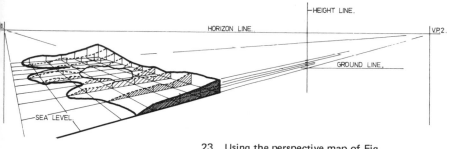

23 Using the perspective map of Fig. 22, heights (taken from contour lines) can be located at each intersection of the grid lines. This will allow sections to be set up along the grid lines, as shown, from which an accurate three-dimensional view can be drawn.

complex shapes, can be shown accurately in a perspective drawing.

To obtain the most from any of the methods described in this book it is necessary for the student to use his powers of observation and his imagination when approaching any subject with a view to producing a perspective drawing of it. This will usually reward him handsomely in economy of time and in the high degree of accuracy obtained in the final drawing.

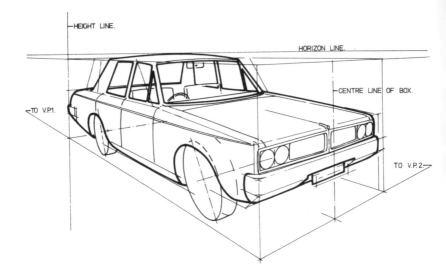

24　Perspective drawing of an automobile, with
the original 'box' indicated.

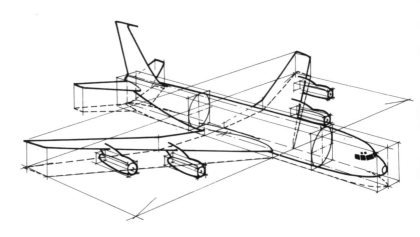

25　A modern jet aircraft drawn in perspective,
with the 'box' outlines indicated. Details have
been omitted, to show the method of construction more clearly.

4 The box method

It is said, 'If you can draw a rectangular prism in perspective you can draw anything man can make.' This sounds at first like a gross exaggeration or the boast of a self-opinionated delineator trying to impress a prospective client. However, if the statement is examined a little more closely, and in conjunction with various problems, its basic truth becomes apparent.

By referring to the section on drawing regular and irregular shapes in perspective (Fig. 16) it will be found that if a pentagon is enclosed in a square, or 'put in a box', it can be drawn in one-point or two-point perspective in the normal way. In other words, the problem becomes a simple matter of a square box on which certain points are located; the required object is then drawn by joining up these points and removing the box.

The automobile is one object which has always caused the student a great deal of trouble in a perspective construction. However, if the automobile is placed in a box the only problem is to draw a rectangular prism. Once this rectangular prism has been drawn in perspective it remains only to remove parts of the box to obtain the general shape of the automobile (Fig. 24). From this point the degree of refinement is a matter of personal choice but the method for obtaining an accurate shape is based on the assumption that if you can draw a basic rectangular prism (box) you can draw any type of automobile. This still holds true even as the design of the automobile becomes more and more sleek in accordance with the current theories of aerodynamics.

This 'basic box' idea remains true even when drawing such complex shapes as modern jet aircraft. Again, if the aircraft is contained in a box and parts of the box removed according to the dimensions of the aircraft, what is left is an accurate perspective drawing of the aircraft (Fig. 25).

The types of objects with more or less complex shapes that can be fitted into a simple rectangular prism for the purpose of drawing them in perspective are almost endless and include such objects as boats, ships, railway rolling stock, buses, road transport, machinery of all types, sculpture, equipment, furniture and fittings. Of these, the most common items with which the student has difficulty is the chair. In perspective drawing the chair is greatly simplified if it is first placed in a box from which pieces are cut out until the required shape of the chair remains. Fig. 26 shows the method of using the box for both a simple chair and a slightly more complex one. Without the box even the simple chair is difficult to draw in perspective but once the problem becomes a basic rectangular prism it is greatly simplified, and removing parts of the box to leave the required chair shape is a comparatively easy exercise. In other words, 'if you can draw a rectangular prism in perspective you can draw anything man can make.'

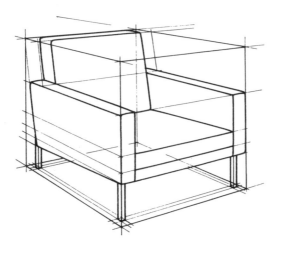

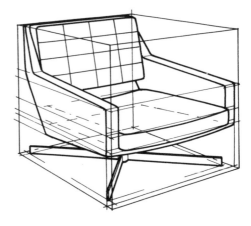

26   The 'box' method applied to two chairs.

5 Circles, cylinders and spheres

Perhaps the most difficult of all shapes to handle accurately in perspective drawing is the circle. The only time a true circle is seen in perspective drawing is when it is located parallel to the picture plane, i.e. at right-angles to the centre line of vision, and as this very seldom occurs it can almost be discounted. Except for this rare occurrence, it is seen in a perspective drawing as an ellipse or a straight line. When a circle which is located at right-angles to the picture plane and parallel to the centre line of vision coincides with the centre line of vision it is seen by the spectator as a straight line (Fig. 27), either horizontal or vertical depending on whether the circle is parallel to the ground plane or at right-angles to it. As the circle is moved further away from the centre line of vision, in any direction, without changing its angle to either the ground or the picture plane, the spectator sees more of the face of the circle. That is to say the circle appears to him as an ellipse which increases in width as it is placed further from the centre line of vision.

At this point the student needs to understand something about the ellipse as a geometric figure in order to understand how it is handled in perspective drawing. An ellipse is an oval figure constructed on two unequal axes, a major axis and a minor axis, which always bisect each other at right-angles. The ellipse consists of four identical quadrants, as shown in Fig. 28. The only other fact which need be known at this stage is that an ellipse can always be contained in a rectangle. An ellipse is among the more difficult figures for the student to attempt and the few instruments that are available for drawing ellipses are somewhat expensive. This makes it necessary for the student to look at the various other methods which can be used for drawing ellipses.

When using a freehand line to draw an ellipse it is necessary first to set up the major and the minor axes and also the rectangle which will contain the final ellipse. Fig. 29 shows the steps required for drawing a freehand ellipse and also the finished ellipse. A great deal

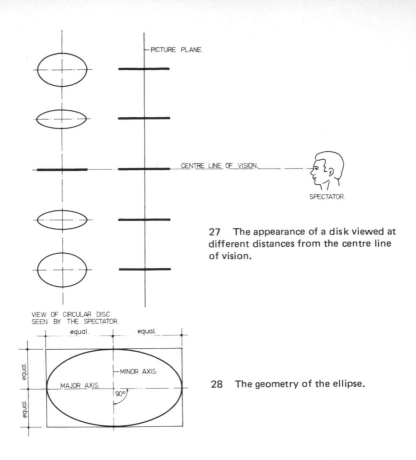

PICTURE PLANE.

CENTRE LINE OF VISION.

SPECTATOR.

27   The appearance of a disk viewed at different distances from the centre line of vision.

VIEW OF CIRCULAR DISC SEEN BY THE SPECTATOR.

equal.   equal.

MINOR AXIS.

MAJOR AXIS.   90°

equal   equal

28   The geometry of the ellipse.

of practice is needed before acceptable ellipses can be produced in this way and a modification of this method will probably achieve better results for the student. This modification, shown in Fig. 30, consists of the same basic set-up of the major and minor axes together with the rectangle surrounding the ellipse. The next step consists of the accurate drawing of one quadrant only of the ellipse. A tracing is then taken of the quadrant, the major and the minor axes and the quarter of the rectangle to be used as reference. Using the tracing the other three quadrants of the ellipse can be drawn to complete the ellipse. Again, practice is necessary before good ellipses are produced.

There are a number of other methods which can be used to produce an ellipse. Though some of these methods still rely on a freehand line finally to draw the ellipse they are considered more accurate than the freehand methods shown in Figs 29 and 30 because more points on the curve of the ellipse are located. The method shown in

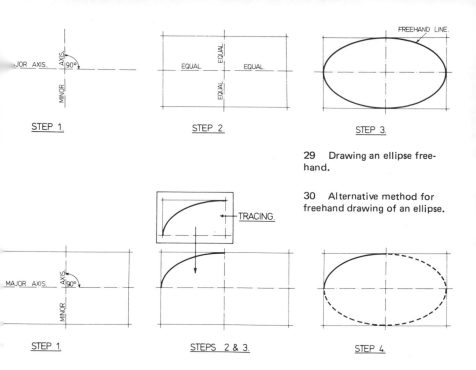

STEP 1. STEP 2. STEP 3.

29 Drawing an ellipse free-hand.

30 Alternative method for freehand drawing of an ellipse.

STEP 1. STEPS 2 & 3. STEP 4.

Fig. 31 is one where the points on the curve are located by the intersection of lines. Half of the major axis is divided into a number of equal parts (four in this case). Half one end of the rectangle containing the ellipse is also divided into the same number of equal parts. From point A lines are drawn through the divisions of the major axis and from point B through the divisions of the end of the rectangle. The curve of the ellipse is then drawn using a freehand line through the intersections of these lines. The other three quadrants can be constructed in the same way or the completed quadrant can be traced as previously described and the ellipse can be completed with the aid of the tracing.

The method shown in Fig. 32 is known as the trammel method and is one of the most favoured because it avoids a mass of construction lines which are required by some of the other methods. This method requires the setting up of the minor and major axes. A straight strip of card or stout paper (a trammel) is placed along the major axis and half the length of the major axis is marked along the trammel. From the same end of the trammel half the length of the minor axis is also marked. The trammel is placed on the drawing so that the two marks separated by the difference between the two halves of the axes fall on the major and minor axes

37

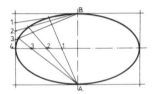

31 Drawing an ellipse by intersection of lines.

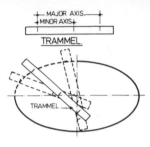

32 Drawing an ellipse: the trammel
method.

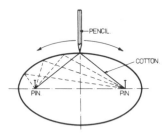

33 Drawing an ellipse with pins and
cotton.

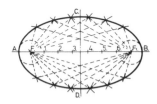

34 . Drawing an ellipse: freehand
method by arcs from the foci.

as shown. The trammel is moved so that the two marks on it always
coincide with the two axes of the ellipse while the third mark on the
trammel is used to locate points on the curve of the ellipse. As
many points as required can be located in this way. The ellipse is
completed by drawing a freehand line through the points located
with the aid of the trammel.

Another simple method for drawing ellipses is shown in Fig. 33.
This method consists of using two pins and a length of cotton. The
two pins are located on the major axis at equal distances from each
end. (This method also requires the setting up of the major and
the minor axes as the first step.) The piece of cotton is then either
tied or looped around the two pins with sufficient slack to allow
a pencil point to coincide with one end of the minor axis when the
cotton is held taut. The ellipse is drawn by moving the pencil around
with the cotton held taut against it.

The method shown in Fig. 34 is based on a similar principle to
the previous one but arcs of a circle are used to locate the points on
the curve of the ellipse. The ellipse is a continuous line following a
curve in such a way that the sum of the distances from any point
in the curved line to two fixed points (foci) on the major axis remains

38

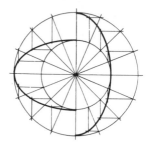

35 Drawing an ellipse: the concentric circle method.

constant. Reference to Fig. 33, in which the piece of cotton remained the same length throughout the exercise, will help the student to understand this principle. In this method as with each of the others the major and the minor axes are located first. The fixed points (foci) are located by swinging an arc from point C with a radius equal to half the length of the major axis to meet the major axis at F and F_1. The distance between these two fixed points is then divided into an odd number of equal parts (7 in this example). Using fixed point F as the centre an arc is drawn with a diameter equal to the distance from A to point 1. Arcs can then be drawn through each of the divisions using point F as the centre. Using fixed point F_1, arcs are again drawn through each of the divisions. By drawing a freehand line through the intersections of the arcs drawn from points F and F_1 the ellipse can be completed.

Fig. 35, the final method to be dealt with here, uses two circles with a common centre. The diameter of the larger circle is equal to the length of the major axis and the diameter of the smaller one is equal to the length of the minor axis. A convenient number of radials are drawn cutting the circumferences of both circles and from these points lines are drawn parallel to the axes. The intersections of these lines locate points on the curve of the ellipse which is drawn by using a freehand line to join the points.

Although the previous examples illustrate a number of methods which can be used for setting up ellipses it should be noted that the methods used here are by no means all that are available to the student. However, the ones shown should be sufficient for the purpose of studying circles, cylinders and spheres in perspective.

One of the most valuable aids in drawing ellipses is the ellipse template. However, ellipse templates have one serious limitation: each template has only a limited number of sizes and projections, which means that the student must have access to a large number of templates, but because of the expense involved this is seldom possible. Therefore it is necessary for him to develop his ability to draw ellipses using less expensive methods.

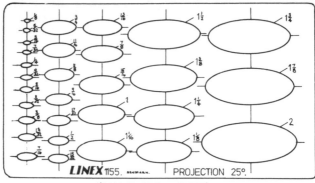

36 Ellipse template.

(HALF FULL SIZE)

Once the drawing of the ellipse has been mastered it is possible to proceed to the circle in perspective drawing. A true circle can always be surrounded by a true square. If the diagonals of the square are drawn they will pass through the centre of the circle. A true square can also be constructed within a true circle and, similarly, its diagonals will pass through the centre of the circle. Fig. 37 shows a true circle with a true square surrounding it and another constructed within its circumference. This knowledge is very important when circles are to be drawn in perspective because it is necessary first to enclose a circle in a framework of straight lines, so that the framework can be set up in perspective. The points where the curve meets the framework in the plan can be located in the perspective construction and from these the view of the circle in the perspective can be drawn.

In Fig. 38, which shows a plan view of a spectator looking at a circle, it can be seen that, to the spectator, the diameter appears shorter than a line joining the points where the spectator's visual rays meet the circumference of the circle. This line joining the extremities of the circumference of the circle as seen by the spectator must be the major axis of the ellipse which the spectator sees. This means that when a circle is viewed in perspective the major axis does not, as might be expected, coincide with the diameter of the circle. Fig. 39 shows the view of the circle seen by the spectator in Fig. 38 and demonstrates the fact that the centre of the circle cannot coincide with the intersection of the major and the minor axes of the ellipse but falls behind the major axis and in the minor axis. The foreshortening of the two halves of the circle is clearly evident in this figure, which is consistent with the basic principles of perspective projection.

40

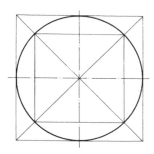

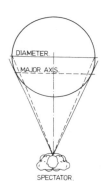

37   The geometry of the circle.

38   Looking obliquely at a circle, showing how the major axis of the resultant ellipse is arrived at.

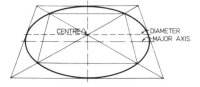

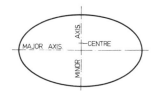

39   The spectator's view of the circle in Fig. 38.

The method used for setting up a perspective view of a circle using a one-point construction relies on the fact that a true circle can be enclosed in a true square. Fig. 40 shows the plan of a circle prepared for perspective drawing with a square constructed around the circle with the vertical and horizontal axes and the diagonals drawn. Once this plan of the circle has been prepared the problem is simply one of drawing a square in perspective, using one-point construction. Fig. 41 shows the method. Once the square is drawn in the perspective view, complete with the vertical and horizontal axes and the diagonals, visual rays can be drawn through the points where the circumference of the circle intersects the axes and diagonals in the plan. These points can then be projected up and located in the perspective view. By joining these points with a freehand line the ellipse (the view of the circle in perspective) can be drawn.

Fig. 42 shows the method used for drawing the circle in perspective using a two-point construction. Once the plan is prepared as in Fig. 40 the object to be set up becomes a square which can be set up in the normal way. The points of intersection of the circumference

41

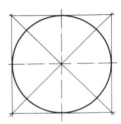

40 Circle prepared for perspective drawing.

41 Drawing a circle in one-point perspective.

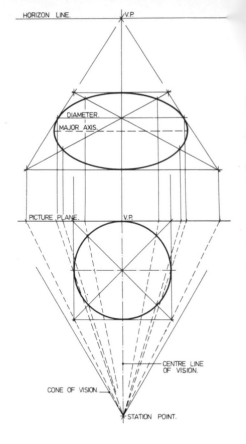

on the axes and the diagonals are located in the perspective view in the same way as they were located in Fig. 41. The ellipse is then drawn by joining these points of intersection with a freehand line.

In Figs. 41 and 42 the centre line of vision passes through the centre of the circle, i.e. the centre line of vision coincides with the minor axis of the ellipse. If the subject of a perspective drawing consists of a number of circles as shown in Fig. 43 this is no longer the case. Rather it is no longer the case for the two outer circles although the middle one still conforms because its centre coincides with the centre line of vision.

It is at this point that one of the anomalies of perspective projection occurs because if the normal method of construction is used, as shown in Fig. 44, the two circles whose centres do not fall in the centre line of vision appear different from the one whose centre does coincide with it. When the two outer circles are examined it can be seen that their major and minor axes are no longer horizontal and

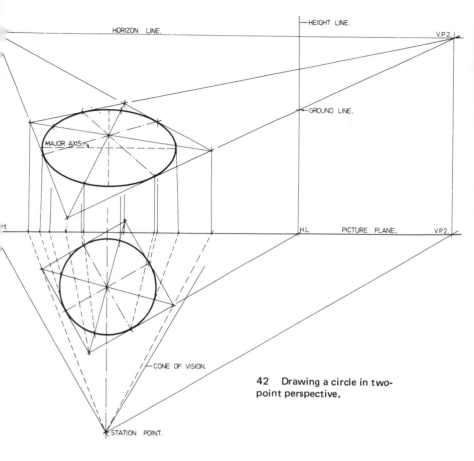

HORIZON LINE.

HEIGHT LINE.

V.P.2.

GROUND LINE.

MAJOR AXIS.

H.L. PICTURE PLANE. V.P.2.

CONE OF VISION.

STATION POINT.

42 Drawing a circle in two-point perspective.

43 Three circles seen from one station point.

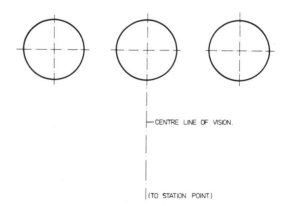

CENTRE LINE OF VISION.

(TO STATION POINT.)

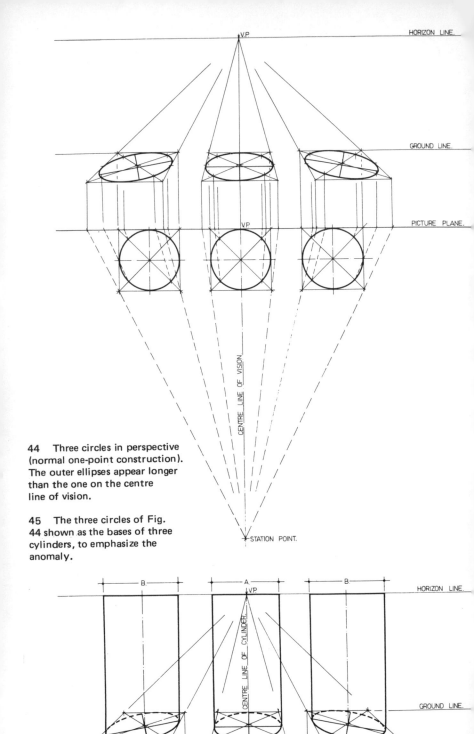

HORIZON LINE.

V.P

GROUND LINE.

PICTURE PLANE.

V.P.

CENTRE LINE OF VISION

STATION POINT.

44 Three circles in perspective
(normal one-point construction).
The outer ellipses appear longer
than the one on the centre
line of vision.

45 The three circles of Fig.
44 shown as the bases of three
cylinders, to emphasize the
anomaly.

B — A — B

HORIZON LINE.
V.P

CENTRE LINE OF CYLINDER

GROUND LINE.

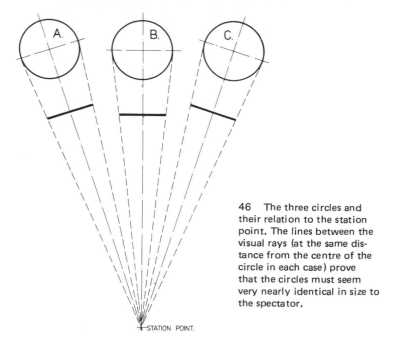

46 The three circles and their relation to the station point. The lines between the visual rays (at the same distance from the centre of the circle in each case) prove that the circles must seem very nearly identical in size to the spectator.

STATION POINT.

vertical and in fact the ellipses representing these circles as seen by the spectator appear larger than the middle one. If these three circles are considered as the bases of three cylinders (Fig. 45) it can be seen clearly that the cylinders on either side of the middle one appear distorted. In addition they appear wider than the middle one, which means that they must be closer to the spectator than the middle one. Simple observation of the diagram shows that this cannot be so: therefore the solution shown in Fig. 45 is contrary to the laws of perspective. (Things appear to become smaller as the distance between them and the spectator increases.) Furthermore, the outer sides of the outer cylinders appear to be longer than the sides adjacent to the middle cylinder which again is a contradiction of the laws of perspective.

Fig. 46 shows that the spectator in fact sees three cylinders as being virtually the same size. The line between the visual rays in each case is located at the same distance from the centre of each circle. The difference in distances between the spectator and the cylinders is very small in this example and for all practical purposes can be disregarded. However, it could reasonably be argued that the distance between the two outer cylinders and the spectator is very slightly greater than the distance between the spectator and the middle one. This would mean that, in theory, the two outer ones

45

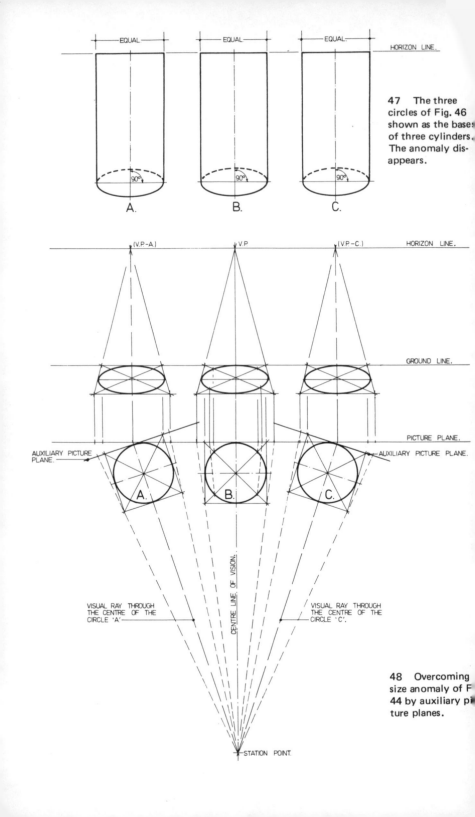

47 The three circles of Fig. 46 shown as the bases of three cylinders. The anomaly disappears.

HORIZON LINE.

EQUAL · EQUAL · EQUAL

90° · 90° · 90°

A. · B. · C.

(V.P.-A.) · V.P. · (V.P.-C.) HORIZON LINE.

GROUND LINE.

PICTURE PLANE.

AUXILIARY PICTURE PLANE. AUXILIARY PICTURE PLANE.

A. · B. · C.

CENTRE LINE OF VISION.

VISUAL RAY THROUGH THE CENTRE OF THE CIRCLE 'A'

VISUAL RAY THROUGH THE CENTRE OF THE CIRCLE 'C'.

STATION POINT.

48 Overcoming size anomaly of Fig 44 by auxiliary picture planes.

should be slightly smaller than the middle one, not larger as they appear in Fig. 45.

Before proceeding further at this stage it is necessary to examine a little more closely what is seen by a spectator when he looks at a circle. It is a fact that a number of spectators looking at a circle from different directions, provided they are all at the same distance from the circle and have the same eye-level, will see the same shape, i.e. an identical ellipse. Additionally, a spectator looking at a number of circles equidistant from him will see the same shape for each of them because, no matter where he stands to look at the circles, so long as his eye-level and his distance from the circles remain constant he will see the same shape. Many authorities appear to become confused on this point and in the past few, if any, have discovered the answer to the anomaly in Fig. 44.

The statement that a circle looked at from any angle will appear as the same shape, provided the distance between the spectator and the circle and his eye-level remain constant is the key to answering this question once and for all. In the light of the foregoing, Fig. 47 shows the three cylinders as they will appear to the spectator. Before leaving this explanation it is worth pointing out that further proof of the answer given in Fig. 47 can be obtained by referring to *Basic Perspective,* and specifically the part dealing with one-point perspective.

It has been shown in Figs. 44 and 45 that a correct result cannot be obtained by using the normal perspective construction: therefore it is necessary to overcome this anomaly by modifying the construction so that the correct results are obtained. There are a number of ways in which this can be done, the simplest method being the introduction of an 'auxiliary picture plane' for each of the circles whose centre does not coincide with the centre line of vision of the main perspective construction. This method is shown in Fig. 48 where, in each of the cases in which the centre of the circle does not coincide with the centre line of vision, a visual ray is drawn through the centre and, using this ray in a similar way to the centre line of vision, an auxiliary picture plane is drawn at right-angles to it at the same distance from the centre of the circle as the main picture plane. Circle *B* has its centre coinciding with the centre line of vision and can be drawn in the 'normal' way. Circles *A* and *C* are drawn using auxiliary picture planes with the squares constructed around them in the directions of the visual rays through their centres and the auxiliary picture planes as shown. The points are then located on the auxiliary picture plane and transferred to the main picture plane by measurement either side of the intersection of the visual ray through the

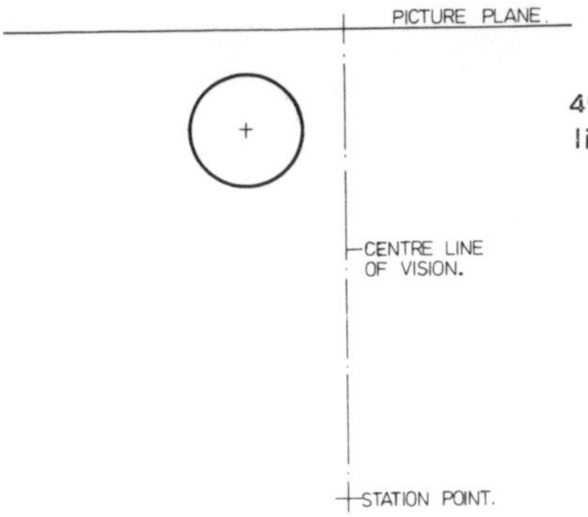

PICTURE PLANE

49　A circle occurring off the centre line of vision.

CENTRE LINE OF VISION.

STATION POINT.

centre of the circle and the main picture plane. This locates the circle accurately in the over-all perspective construction and from this point forward the construction is exactly the same as for circle *B*.

From Fig. 48 it can be seen that when the centre of a circle in a perspective construction does not coincide with the centre line of vision, irrespective of whether the main construction is one-point or two-point, the circle can be drawn within the construction using a simple one-point construction and an auxiliary picture plane.

The results obtained in Fig. 48 show that the spectator will see the three circles as the same shape and because the variation in distance between the spectator and the circles is negligible they will appear to be the same size. For all practical purposes this variation in distance is so small that it can safely be ignored. In this example the spectator is looking at three identical circles from virtually the same distance and with the same eye-level so the three cylinders will give the correct answer (see Fig. 47). Because this answer is at variance with most printed works on the principles of the circle in perspective projection the method is shown in Figs. 49 and 50. Fig. 49 shows a circle occurring in any perspective construction in which the centre of the circle does not fall in the centre line of vision. Fig. 50 shows the six steps required to draw a perspective view of the circle. The steps are:

Step 1. From the station point draw a visual ray through the centre of the circle to meet the picture plane.

Step 2. Construct a square around the circle using the visual ray as the main axis (vertical axis when the centre line of vision passes through the centre of the circle). Locate the other axis at right-angles to this one and then locate the diagonals.

Step 3. Locate the auxiliary picture plane at right-angles to the visual ray through the centre of the circle, the same distance from the centre of the circle as the main picture plane.

Step 4. Project up from the intersection of the visual ray through the centre of the circle and the main picture plane and locate in the horizon line a vanishing point for the square around the circle (already located for the main construction). Also project the two sides of the square parallel to the central visual ray back to the auxiliary picture plane; these are then transferred by measurement to the main picture plane where they are located at the correct distance on either side of the intersection of the main picture plane and the central visual ray. These two points are then projected up to the ground line.

)a   Drawing a perspective view of the circle in
g. 49. Steps 1-4.

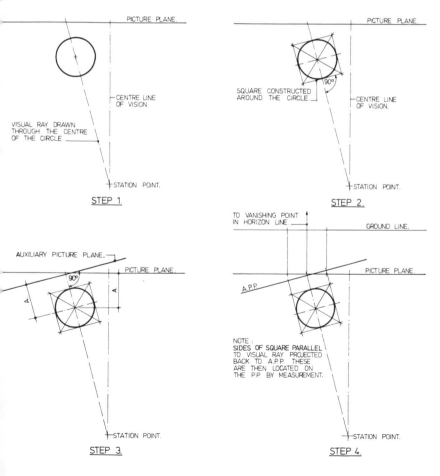

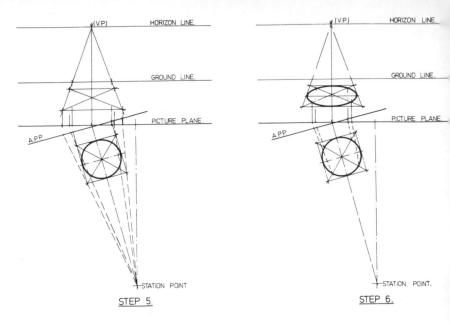

HORIZON LINE.

(V.P)

HORIZON LINE.

(V.P)

GROUND LINE.

GROUND LINE.

PICTURE PLANE.

PICTURE PLANE

A.P.P

A.P.P

STATION POINT

STATION POINT.

STEP 5.

STEP 6.

50*b* Drawing a perspective view of the circle in
Fig. 49. Steps 5 and 6.

Step 5. Using the vanishing point for the circle, lines are drawn
through the points (obtained in Step 4) which represent the sides
of the square surrounding the circle in the perspective view. The
square can then be completed in the perspective view by sighting
the required corners, which are transferred to the main picture
plane and projected up in the normal way. The diagonals can then
be drawn simply by joining the opposite corners of the square in
the perspective view.

Step 6. The intersections of the circumference of the circle and the
diagonals are sighted and the points located on the auxiliary
picture plane; from here they are transferred to the main picture
plane, where they can be projected up to locate these intersections in the perspective view. The ellipse, i.e. the view of the
circle in perspective, can then be drawn through these points.

Once the shape of the circle is drawn in perspective the auxiliary
picture plane which was introduced to enable the correct shape to be
obtained is of no further use. To obtain points on the circumference
of the circle or within it the main picture plane is used in the normal
way. Fig. 51 shows the method used for locating points *A, B,* and *C*

50

on the circumference of the circle in their correct relationship to the circle as seen by the spectator located at the station point. From this it can be seen that nothing changes in the final perspective view except that if the auxiliary picture plane is used to draw the shape of the circle as seen by the spectator it will result in a correct representation of what he will see as opposed to an incorrect representation if it is not used.

From the foregoing explanation of the method used to produce perspectives of circles it can be seen that cylinders follow the same basic rules. Fig. 52 shows the construction of a cylinder when the centre line of vision does not pass through the main axis of the cylinder. From the previous explanation it can be seen that the major axis of an ellipse, which is the result of viewing a circle in the horizontal plane, will always be horizontal, i.e. it will always be at right-angles to the main axis of the cylinder of which it can be said to form an end. In this case the main axis of the cylinder will be vertical, which means that the minor axis of the ellipse will coincide with the main axis of the cylinder. It is this fact which explains the most important rule to remember when drawing circles in perspective, regardless of whether they fall in the horizontal or vertical plane: *The major axis of the ellipse will always be at right-angles to the main axis of the*

51 Locating points on the circumference of a circle drawn in perspective.

52 Perspective construction of a cylinder whose main axis lies off the centre line of vision.

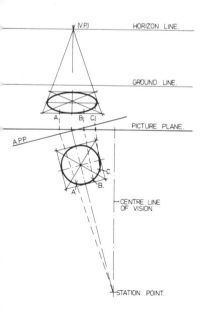

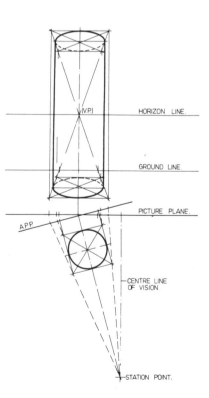

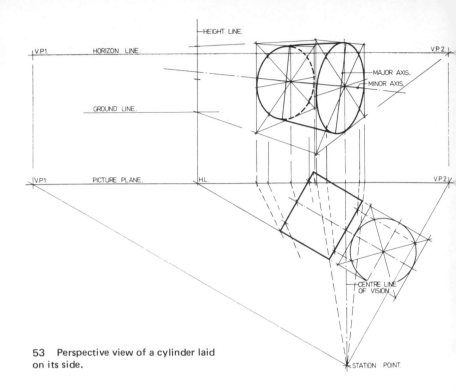

53 Perspective view of a cylinder laid on its side.

cylinder of which it can be said to form an end. Therefore the minor axis will always coincide with this main axis and the centre of the circle will always fall in the minor axis behind the intersection of the major and minor axes. If this basic rule is remembered circles will cause the delineator very little trouble.

In Fig. 53 the main axis of the cylinder is horizontal, i.e. parallel to the ground, and its ends are in a vertical plane, which means that it will 'vanish' to V.P.1. Because the major axis of the ellipse is always at right-angles to the main axis of the cylinder it will no longer be vertical. If the square surrounding the circle is constructed in the normal way, together with the diagonals and the vertical and horizontal axes, each end of the cylinder can be located in the perspective view by simple projection or at least the squares containing the ends of the cylinder can be located. Next it is necessary to locate the intersections of the circumference and the diagonals in the plan so that they can be located in the perspective view. But these intersections cannot be located immediately in the plan because the circular ends appear as straight lines and therefore it is necessary to set up an elevation. If this is set up in the correct relationship to the plan (as shown) it can save a good deal of extra work. The intersections of the circumference and the diagonals can be projected directly onto the plan, and from there they can be located in the perspective view. The perspective view of the ends of the cylinder can then be drawn by producing an ellipse through the points of intersection of the circumference of the circle and the diagonals and the vertical and horizontal axes of the circular ends.

Because circles and cylinders are so similar in their construction in perspective drawing it is unnecessary to study cylinders further at this stage. However, one variation to the method already shown is of use for drawing circles in perspective when they occur in a horizontal plane. The variation consists of enclosing the circle in a trapezium instead of the square used in the previous examples. Fig. 54 shows the construction when the circle is enclosed in a trapezium in which two sides coincide with the visual rays forming tangents to the circle. The other two sides of the trapezium are drawn parallel with the picture plane, or with the auxiliary picture plane when the centre of the circle does not coincide with the centre line of vision of the main construction. The diagonals in this case will not intersect in the centre of the circle but instead will locate the major axis of the resulting ellipse, i.e. the major axis will fall in a straight line between the two tangent points of the visual rays used to construct the trapezium. The perspective view of this particular trapezium in this location will be a rectangle and when its diagonals are located the major axis can be drawn parallel to the ground line. The points of intersection of the circumference of the circle and the diagonals are located in the perspective in the usual way and the ellipse is shown by drawing a line through all of the relevant points.

The method of construction is the same for both circles except that an auxiliary picture plane must be used for circle *B*. The actual centre of the circle is not located in this method unless further steps are used. In order to locate the centre of the circle in the perspective view it is necessary to construct at least two diagonally opposite corners of a square which will contain the plan of the circle. These two corners can then be located in the perspective view as shown and a diagonal line drawn. It is already known that this diagonal will intersect the minor axis of the ellipse in the perspective position of the true centre of the circle.

The development of this method is so similar to the 'square' method that it is not taken any further here but those who are attracted to this method rather than the 'square' should note that it

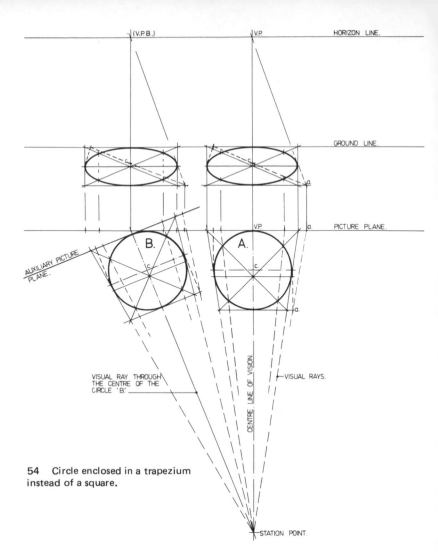

54 Circle enclosed in a trapezium instead of a square.

can be used not only for circles but for those cylinders whose ends fall in a horizontal plane.

Once the circle and the cylinder in perspective projection are understood the sphere can be drawn in perspective with very little trouble. The basic theory of the sphere is very similar to that of the circle and the cylinder although it is a little more complicated to draw. The explanation of the method is shown in Fig. 55 where an elevation has been set up in a similar way to the ones used in three-point perspective constructions. From this it can be seen that the plan and the elevation have squares constructed around the sphere

in each view. This has the effect of putting the sphere in a 'box',
which is consistent with the methods for drawing other complex
shapes. The box containing the sphere can be set up in the perspective
view in the usual way. Once this is done it is possible to locate the
diagonals on the base of the box and on these to locate their intersections with the circumference of the plan of the sphere. Next the
plan of the sphere, which will of course be an ellipse, can be drawn
in the perspective view. The major axis of this ellipse can be located
(through the middle of the ellipse). Where this major axis intersects
the sides of the square in the perspective view are the tangent points
formed by the visual rays i.e. the furthest edges of the view of the
sphere seen by the spectator. In other words, this will be the diameter
of the sphere in the perspective view or, to be more accurate at this
stage, it will be the width of the sphere through its centre. Because
of this it is necessary to locate a horizontal plane through the centre
of the sphere as shown in Fig. 55. The diagonals of this square plane
through the centre of the sphere will intersect in the true centre of
the sphere.

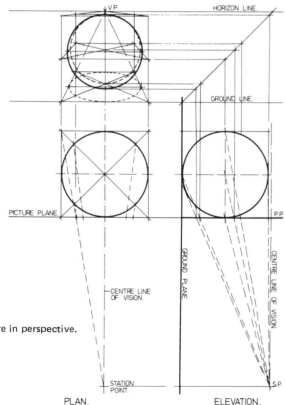

55 Drawing a sphere in perspective.

PLAN.   ELEVATION.

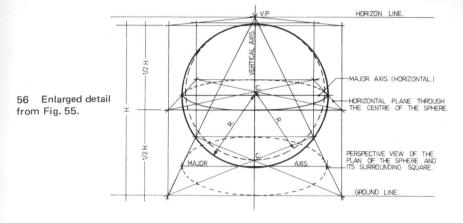

56   Enlarged detail
from Fig. 55.

At this stage it is necessary to clarify exactly what we see when we look at a sphere. From the previous section about circles it can be said that a spectator looking at a sphere from any angle will see the same shape. It is not necessary to go into further explanation of this point because the arguments have been discussed previously. However, exactly what that shape is that the spectator sees from any angle is extremely important when drawing spheres in perspective.

It is a common assumption that the shape he sees is a perfect circle. If this were the case it would be necessary to construct the circle using the centre of the sphere located by constructing the horizontal plane through its centre. If this is attempted it will soon be learned that the circle drawn using this centre is in fact a circle representing the horizontal axis of the plan of the sphere. This cannot be the shape seen by the spectator because this line coincides with the diameter of the circle seen in plan and this possibility has already been eliminated (see Fig. 38, p. 41). In fact the spectator cannot see a true circle when he looks at a sphere.

The only other logical alternative is that he sees an ellipse. If this is so, then the centre of the ellipse is the intersection of the major and minor axes. Mathematics tells us that a circle is only a special kind of ellipse; therefore what the spectator sees is not a circle but a circular ellipse i.e. an ellipse in which the two foci coincide. It follows that the shape seen by the spectator can be drawn with a compass, using the intersection of the major and the minor axes and a radius equal to half the length of the major axis. This may seem at first sight like splitting hairs but if the foregoing facts are checked against the introduction to this chapter (p. 35) it will be seen that an understanding of them is necessary to the satisfactory understanding of spheres in perspective projection. Fig. 56 is an enlargement of the results achieved in Fig. 55 and should be self-explanatory. An elevation of the construction was included in Fig. 55 to help in the explanation of constructing a perspective view of a sphere but it can be readily seen that this elevation is not necessary for the construction.

Of the two spheres in Fig. 57, sphere *A,* which has its centre in the centre line of vision, is drawn in perspective using the 'square' method. Once the square is set up in the perspective view the horizontal plane can be located by measurement on the picture plane and its diagonals drawn. The intersections of the circumference and the diagonals can be located, by projection from the plan, on the

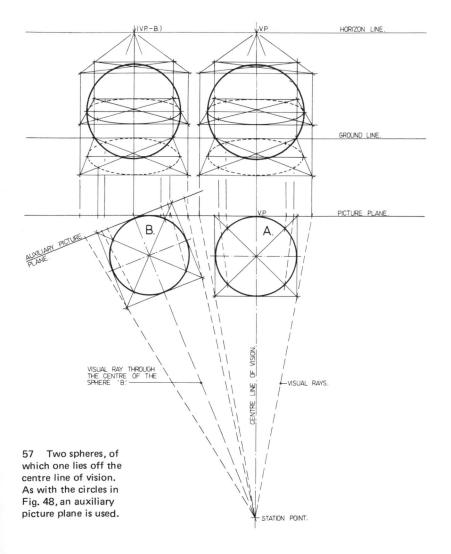

57   Two spheres, of which one lies off the centre line of vision. As with the circles in Fig. 48, an auxiliary picture plane is used.

diagonals of both the base plane and the central plane of the box. In any perspective view of a sphere which is intended to form the basis of a rendering it is important that the plan view of the sphere be located on the base plane of the box. The reason for this will be made clear in the chapter on shadow projection; sufficient here to say that it is necessary and can be done with very little extra work at this stage. Once the major axis is located by measurement the line of the ellipse can be drawn on these two planes. Using the intersection of the major and the minor axes as the centre and a radius of half the major axis the sphere can be drawn in the perspective view.

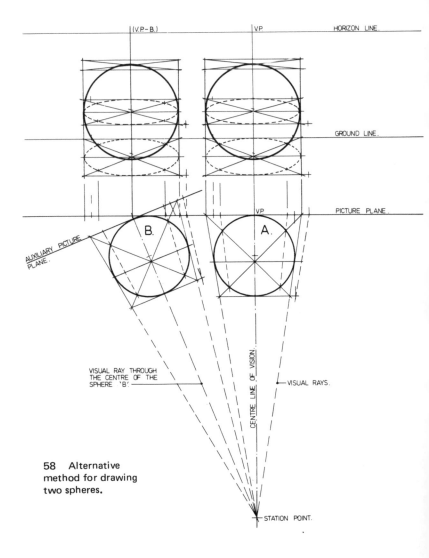

58 Alternative method for drawing two spheres.

Sphere *B* does not have its centre in the centre line of vision, therefore it will be necessary to use an auxiliary picture plane because it can be readily understood that the spectator will see each sphere as the same shape. The actual construction is similar to that for sphere *A* except that all of the points located on the auxiliary picture plane must be transferred by measurement to the main picture plane. Once the shape of the sphere has been drawn in the perspective view the auxiliary picture plane is of no further use and the main picture plane is used to locate points or lines on the surface of the sphere.

Fig. 58 shows an alternative method for drawing the sphere in perspective where sphere *A* has its centre falling in the centre line of vision and sphere *B* does not. This alternative method consists of the use of a trapezium to enclose the plan view of the sphere in the same way as was described in the section dealing with circles. The method will be easily understood by reference to Fig. 58, where it will be seen that it is only a combination of the constructions shown in Figs. 54 and 57.

Fig. 59 shows the method used for locating a horizontal plane through a sphere other than through the centre. The sphere is drawn in the perspective view using the square method described in Fig. 57 (sphere *A*). When this is done it is necessary to set up an elevation of the construction in the usual way. The horizontal plane through the sphere is located on the elevation of the sphere and from this the plan of the sphere at this plane can be drawn on the plan (shown as a broken line on the plan). By means of projections in both the plan and the elevation the plane at this level can be located through the perspective view of the box containing the sphere. The diagonals can be drawn in the usual way. Projections of the intersections of the circumference of the circle on the plane through the sphere with the diagonals in the plan are used to produce the ellipse seen by the spectator when the sphere is cut at this level.

To draw a sphere cut by an inclined plane (Fig. 60), the method is similar to the one described for Fig. 59 so it need not be repeated. However, it should be pointed out that although the plane cutting the box containing the sphere will be inclined, not horizontal, it can easily be located by projections from the elevation.

Fig. 61, the last figure in this chapter, shows the method used for setting up a perspective view of a sphere which has been cut with a vertical plane. The sphere is drawn in the perspective view using the square method and again it is necessary to set up an elevation of the construction in the usual way. The vertical plane cutting the sphere is located on the plan view (in this example it coincides with one of

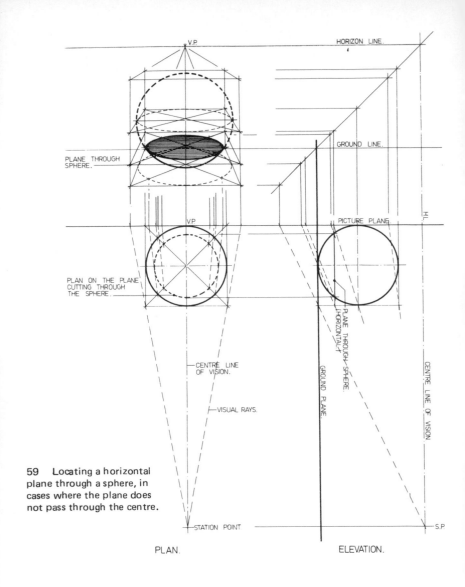

V.P.

HORIZON LINE.

GROUND LINE.

HL

PLANE THROUGH
SPHERE.

V.P.

PICTURE PLANE.

PLAN ON THE PLANE
CUTTING THROUGH
THE SPHERE.

PLANE THROUGH
SPHERE
(HORIZONTAL)

CENTRE LINE
OF VISION.

GROUND PLANE

CENTRE LINE OF VISION

VISUAL RAYS.

59 Locating a horizontal
plane through a sphere, in
cases where the plane does
not pass through the centre.

STATION POINT

S.P

PLAN.

ELEVATION.

the diagonals). This plane through the sphere is then located on the elevation together with its diagonals on which the points of intersection of the circumference of the circle formed by the cut can be located by projection from the plan to enable the ellipse formed by the cut to be drawn in the elevation. The plan and the elevation are used to locate the plane in perspective with its diagonals and the intersections of the circumference of the circle formed by the

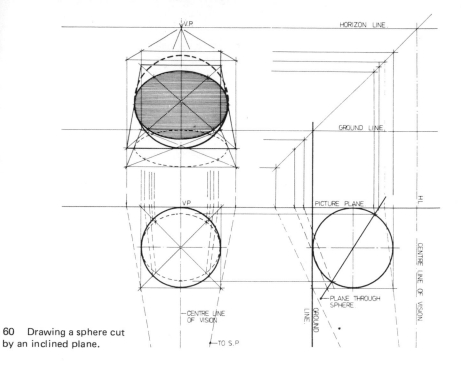

60 Drawing a sphere cut by an inclined plane.

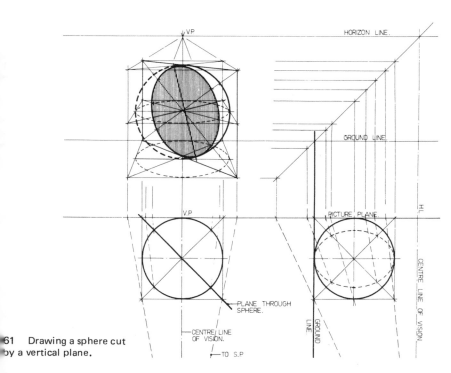

61 Drawing a sphere cut by a vertical plane.

cut. Using these points of intersection, the ellipse which will be seen by the spectator in the circumstances shown here can be drawn in the usual way.

Because of the confusion, in the existing published works, on the whole subject of circles, cylinders and spheres in perspective projection, it should again be emphasized that the solutions described and illustrated here are based on one simple logical fact. When a spectator views a circle in a horizontal plane from any direction, at a constant distance from the circle and a constant eye-level, he will see the circle as an identical ellipse. When viewing a cylinder, of which the axis of symmetry is vertical, from any direction at a constant distance from it and a constant eye-level, he will see the cylinder as an identical shape. When a sphere is viewed from any angle, at a constant distance from it and constant eye-level, it will be seen as an identical shape. Because of this it must be obvious that the basic method of perspective projection is not suitable when the circle, cylinder or sphere does not have its centre falling in the centre line of vision. This anomaly can be overcome by the use of an auxiliary picture plane so that the results obtained are consistent with the logical requirements.

6 Reflections

Reflections occur often in rendering because many surfaces are capable of reflecting images with varying degrees of clarity. Glass in the windows of a building will often reflect images of those things near it, the surface of still water will reflect a mirror image of everything located in the correct relationship to it and even a wet road or pavement will reflect its surroundings. Therefore it is necessary to understand the basic principle of reflection: a reflected image of an object will always appear to be the same distance behind the reflecting surface as the object is in front of it. Fig. 62 shows a rectangular prism placed a short distance from a mirror. The mirror reflects not only the object but the ground or floor between the object and the mirror. It is this which makes the reflection of the object look as though it is the same distance behind the reflecting surface as the object is in front of it. When this is thoroughly understood the construction of reflections in perspective is a simple exercise.

If the reflection of an object will appear to be the same distance behind the reflecting surface as the object is in front of it, then a second or 'image' object can be drawn in the plan (Fig. 63). The object and its reflection can be located in the perspective drawing in the normal way. When the object is a simple rectangular prism, as shown in Fig. 63, this is not a long or involved process. However, if the object is more complicated this method can become unwieldy and then it is necessary to look for a simpler, quicker method of setting up reflections in a perspective drawing. The use of short cuts in perspective drawing enables many long and laborious exercises to be carried out with a minimum expenditure of time and effort. These short cuts are dealt with fully in a later chapter in this book but because one of the basic short cuts is required at this stage it is best to introduce the principle behind it here.

To understand one of the most useful short cuts in perspective projection it is necessary to go back to plane geometry. It is known that the diagonals of a square intersect in the centre of the square

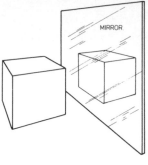

62 Reflection: a rectangular prism, and its image in a mirror.

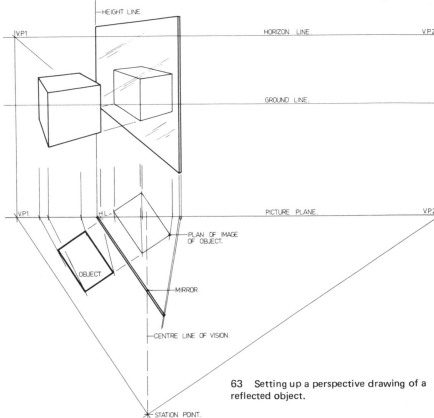

63 Setting up a perspective drawing of a reflected object.

(see Fig. 37), and similarly the diagonals of a rectangle will intersect in the centre of the rectangle. If a square prism and a rectangular prism are set up and drawn in perspective, together with the diagonals on each of the visible faces, these diagonals must still intersect in the centre of each face (Fig. 64). These constructions show that the diagonals locate the centre of each face of each

object in the perspective drawing. In other words, the perspective
drawing shows not only the face of the object but also whatever
is on its surface. Viewing an object from a different position does
not change anything in its surface in reality; therefore, the diagonals
must still intersect in the centre of the square or the rectangle.

Using this centre point of the face of the figure, each face can
be divided into four equal parts in the perspective drawing, as shown
in Fig. 65, which can be checked by projection back to the plan.
Once this is understood, it can be used to advantage in perspective

64 A square prism and a rectangular prism drawn
in perspective, with the diagonals on each of the
visible faces.

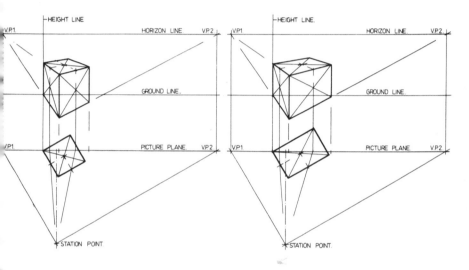

65 Division of each face of a prism into four
equal parts with the help of the diagonals.

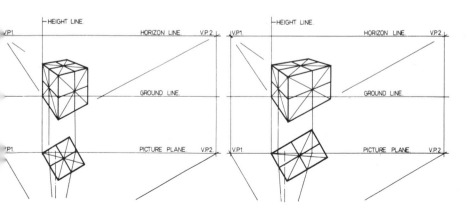

drawing. The principle can be expressed simply: *The diagonals of a square or rectangle can be used to divide the figure exactly in half.* Therefore each half can again be treated as a square or rectangle and be divided in half repeatedly until the object is divided into a great many equal parts. Fig. 66 shows how this can be done using a simple cube. Obviously the rectangular prism can be dealt with in the same way.

This is not the only result which can be obtained from this principle; if it remains true for division of square and rectangular shapes it must remain true for multiplication of the same shapes. Fig. 67 shows a cube which has been set up using a simple two-point perspective construction. To this cube it is required to add more cubes of exactly the same size, which can of course be done by adding more squares to the plan and then projecting them up in the normal way. The same result can be obtained in about half the time by using an adaptation of the principle of diagonals. One face of the cube could be thought of as half of a rectangle which is made up of two identical squares, one of them being a face of the cube under consideration. The diagonals of this rectangle would pass through a point in the middle of a side of the square, as shown in Fig. 67, and if the top and bottom sides of the square were extended as necessary the rectangle equal to two squares could be drawn. This exercise could be repeated many times, resulting in a large number of squares being drawn, each equal in size to the original one. Because this can be done directly in the perspective view without further reference to the plan it is a great time-saver, and because it is based on a geometric fact, it does not suffer any loss of accuracy. This is one of the most valuable short cuts in perspective projection and has

66 Dividing and subdividing the face of a cube.

67 Multiplying a cube by the same principle of diagonals.

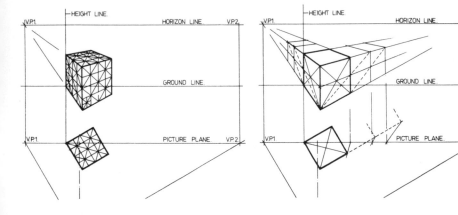

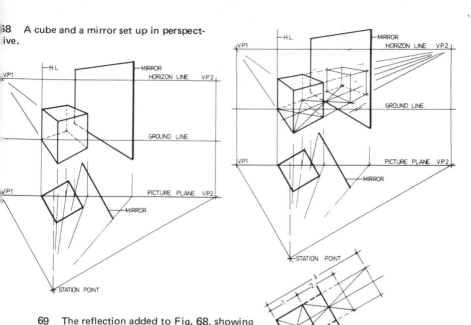

69   The reflection added to Fig. 68, showing
how the diagonals are used to save time and
labour.

a number of other important uses which are dealt with more fully
later. At this stage it is sufficient to understand the basic principle,
which is used to set up reflections without unnecessary work and loss
of time.

If the same cube as used in Figs. 66 and 67 is set up in front of a
mirror in the same way as the rectangular prism was in Fig. 63 it
can be drawn in perspective in the normal way together with the
mirror. However, once the cube and the mirror are drawn in perspective as shown in Fig. 68 the reflection can be completed using
diagonals without further reference to the plan. Fig. 69 shows how
this is done, together with a diagram illustrating the principle involved.
From the example it can be seen that this is a much quicker way than
that shown in Fig. 63, but identical results will be obtained whichever
method is used.

To this stage, the reflecting surface has been placed at right-angles
to the ground plane. Fig. 70 shows a rectangular prism placed on a
horizontal reflecting surface and set up in perspective. The advantage
of using diagonals to locate the reflection can be seen clearly in this
example. If the object is raised above the reflecting surface as shown
in Fig. 71 the diagonals can be used again to advantage and a great

67

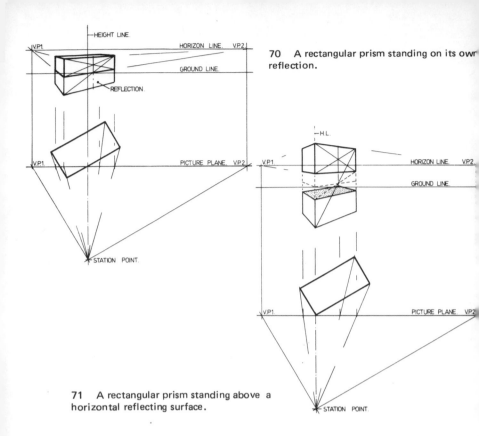

70 A rectangular prism standing on its own reflection.

71 A rectangular prism standing above a horizontal reflecting surface.

deal of time and effort can be saved. Fig. 72 shows one object placed on top of another with the two objects drawn in the perspective view in the normal way. By using diagonals, as shown, the reflections of both of these objects can be located and drawn. If it is remembered that the reflection of an object will appear to be exactly the same distance behind (or below in this example) the reflecting surface as the object is in front (or above) it, this type of subject is fairly simple and straightforward.

There are two sets of conditions which have, as yet, not been discussed. These are a little more complex than the ones dealt with so far because they consist of *(a)* objects and reflecting surfaces which are no longer parallel to each other and *(b)* reflecting surfaces which are neither vertical nor horizontal. The first of these two sets of conditions is shown in Fig. 73 where the reflecting surface is not parallel to a side of the cube. In this example the cube is drawn in the perspective view in the normal way using V.P.1 and V.P.2. The mirror is then drawn, again in the normal way, using V.P.3. Because the reflection of

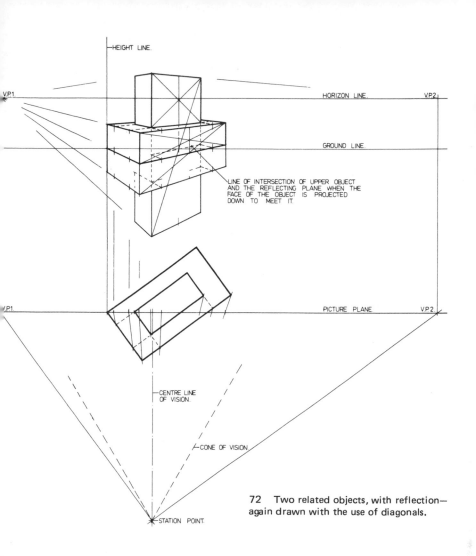

Labels in figure:
HEIGHT LINE.
V.P.1.
HORIZON LINE.
V.P.2.
GROUND LINE.
LINE OF INTERSECTION OF UPPER OBJECT AND THE REFLECTING PLANE WHEN THE FACE OF THE OBJECT IS PROJECTED DOWN TO MEET IT.
V.P.1.
PICTURE PLANE.
V.P.2.
CENTRE LINE OF VISION.
CONE OF VISION.
STATION POINT.

72 Two related objects, with reflection—again drawn with the use of diagonals.

the cube will appear to be the same distance behind the reflecting surface as the object being reflected is in front of it, the plan of the cube representing the reflection can be drawn behind the mirror using the same angles as used for the cube being reflected (see Fig. 63). When this 'second' plan is located in the plan construction its vanishing points can be located in the usual way. By using these vanishing points (V.P.4 and V.P.5) for the 'second' cube in the usual way, the reflection of the cube can be drawn in the perspective view.

The second of these two sets of special conditions occurs in Fig. 74, which shows the method used for locating and drawing the

69

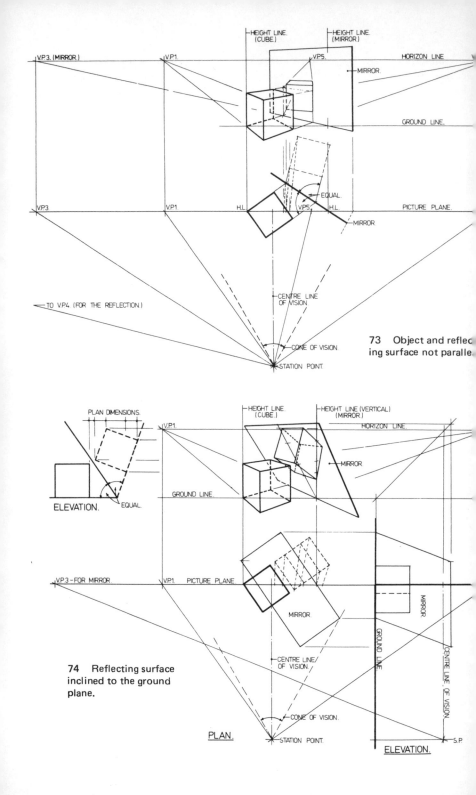

73 Object and reflecting surface not parallel.

74 Reflecting surface inclined to the ground plane.

reflection of a cube when the reflecting surface is inclined to the ground plane, i.e. is neither vertical nor horizontal. This example looks a little more complicated than the previous ones in this chapter because the reflecting surface, which is an inclined plane, requires an elevation of the construction to locate the vertical vanishing point (V.P.3). Once this has been found, both the cube and the mirror are set up and drawn in the perspective view in the normal way. As with the preceding example, it is necessary to locate a plan view of the 'reflection' before it can be located and drawn in the perspective view. To obtain this plan view of the 'reflection', it is necessary to set up an elevation of the cube and the mirror as shown at the left of Fig. 74. This is set up at a convenient distance from the main construction and to save time, as will be seen later, with its ground line coinciding with the ground line of the perspective. Because the object and the reflected image will appear to occupy corresponding respective positions in front of and behind the reflecting surface, an 'elevation of the reflection of the object' can be set up behind the mirror, using equal angles as shown. From this elevation, dimensions can be obtained and used to locate the 'plan of the reflection of the cube' in the plan construction as shown. Once this plan view of the 'reflection of the cube' has been located it is possible to sight its corners and project them up from the picture plane in the normal way. These corners can be located in the perspective view by projecting across horizontally from the previously-prepared elevation to the vertical height line for the mirror. Using V.P.2 these 'heights' on the height line can be located by projection to a line on the inclined surface of the mirror. The reason for this last step should be obvious because the height line used for the mirror is a vertical line and the surface of the mirror is inclined, which means that 'heights' projected across from the elevation must be located on that surface where the reflection will be drawn. The corners of the reflected cube are located using the 'heights' on the inclined line on the surface of the mirror, V.P.1 and the projections up from the plan. This may sound a little complicated at first but, if the basic principles of perspective projection are fully understood, such a reflection as the one described here should not prove difficult when attempted.

To sum up, the most important single fact to remember when dealing with reflections in perspective projection is that the reflection of the object will always appear to be the same distance behind the reflecting surface as the object being reflected is in front of it. If this is learned thoroughly from the very beginning, reflections are quite a simple exercise and need not be time-consuming.

71

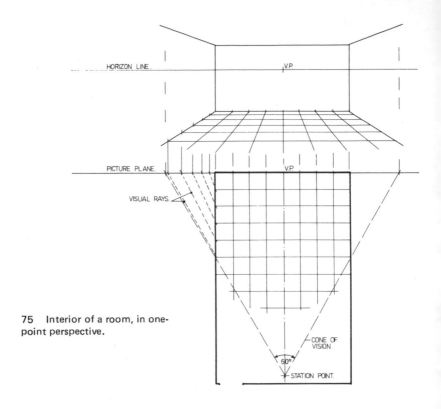

75 Interior of a room, in one-point perspective.

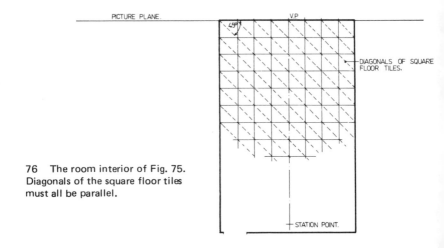

76 The room interior of Fig. 75. Diagonals of the square floor tiles must all be parallel.

7 The use of measuring points

The point known as a measuring point in perspective projection is in reality a vanishing point but, unlike the true vanishing point, which is located by using a sight line parallel to a side or line of an object, a measuring point is located by using a sight line parallel to some construction line, such as a diagonal line of a face of a figure, usually a square or a rectangle.

To explain this more fully, Fig. 75 shows a simple interior of a room set up in perspective using a one-point construction. The floor tiles have been drawn in the perspective view using the normal method of sighting them in the plan and projecting them up to the perspective view. Because these floor tiles are square, diagonals drawn on them will be at an angle of 45° to the picture plane (Fig. 76). Because all of the tiles are the same size and all are square their diagonals will be parallel as shown, therefore they will converge to a common vanishing point in a perspective projection. From Fig. 76 it can be seen that a diagonal drawn from a corner of the room crosses a tile in each 'vertical' and 'horizontal' row until it reaches the opposite wall. It is unnecessary to draw any other diagonals in this method of perspective projection.

Fig. 77 shows the method of setting up the floor tiles using a measuring point. The diagonal drawn will be parallel to all of the other diagonals of the tiles (in this direction). Therefore a vanishing point for these diagonals could be located by drawing a sight line from the station point parallel to the diagonal to meet the picture plane. These diagonals do not exist as a part of the actual view but are in fact construction lines, so this vanishing point is known as a measuring point. Because the end wall of the room in Fig. 77 coincides with the picture plane, the floor tiles can be measured along this wall in the usual way and, by using the vanishing point for the room, the 'vertical' divisions between the tiles can be drawn.

At this stage the knowledge that a diagonal line drawn from the corner of the room will cross a tile in each 'vertical' row and each 'horizontal' row (until it reaches the opposite wall) can be used to

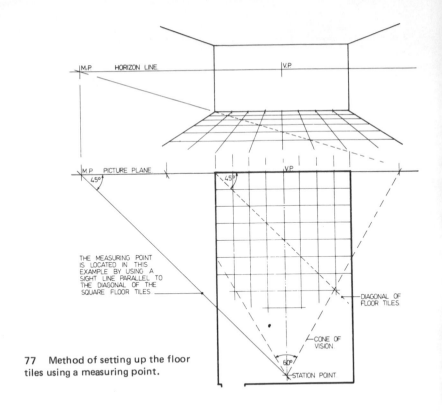

77 Method of setting up the floor tiles using a measuring point.

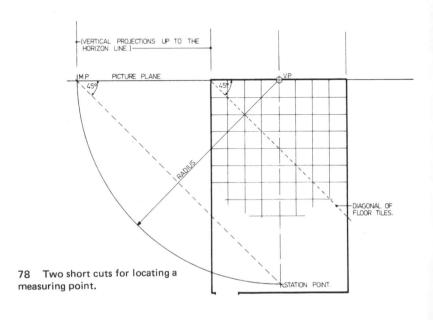

78 Two short cuts for locating a measuring point.

save a considerable amount of time and effort. If the measuring point located in the plan construction is projected up to the horizon line (the diagonals are in the horizontal plane) the diagonal line located in the plan can be located in the perspective view by drawing a line from the measuring point in the horizon line through the appropriate corner of the room until it meets the opposite wall. Where this perspective view of the diagonal line meets the 'vertical' divisions of the floor tiles, will be located the 'horizontal' divisions and therefore the floor tiles can be completed in this view by drawing these in as 'horizontal' lines (i.e. parallel to the picture plane).

Because the diagonals of a square are at 45° to a base line of that square — which, in this example, is parallel to the picture plane — there are a number of alternative short cuts for locating a measuring point. Fig. 78 shows the two most favoured ways, superimposed on the room used for the previous examples. The first of these uses the knowledge that the diagonal of a square tile in this example will be at 45° to the picture plane. Therefore it will not be necessary to do more than draw a line from the station point to meet the picture plane at an angle of 45°. This point of intersection must be the vanishing point for the diagonals of the square floor tiles. The second method for obtaining a measuring point for the diagonals of square floor tiles consists of drawing an arc using the plan position of the vanishing point as the centre and a radius equal to the distance between the vanishing point and the station point. This arc is swung to meet the picture plane and it is this intersection of the arc and the picture plane which is the plan position of the measuring point. When the measuring point is located in the plan it is then projected up to the horizon line in the normal way.

Another method of obtaining a measuring point is not shown but should be obvious from the methods shown so far. This is probably the simplest method of all as it consists simply of measuring the distance between the station point and the vanishing point in the picture plane and transferring this measurement along the horizon line using the vanishing point in the horizon line as the starting point. Regardless of which of the methods shown or described here is used, the principle remains the same and the results obtained will be identical.

The previous examples show a simple use of a measuring point to save time and effort without loss of accuracy. However, the use of a measuring point, or measuring points, is not limited to this type of example only. Measuring points can be used to produce

75

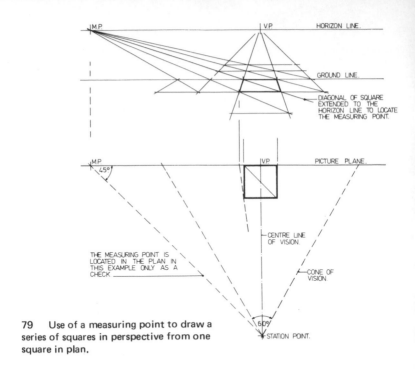

79 Use of a measuring point to draw a series of squares in perspective from one square in plan.

more squares or rectangles, as shown in Fig. 79 where a square is set up in plan in the normal way and the perspective view of it is drawn. If a diagonal is drawn on the perspective view and continued until it intersects the horizon line, this intersection can be used as a measuring point, i.e. the vanishing point for the diagonal of the square and all other lines parallel to it. If any pair of parallel sides of the square are extended, the measuring point can be used to draw another diagonal so that another square of identical size can be added to the first. This can be done using any one of the four sides of the square to add another square or, if necessary, all four sides as shown. The only limitation to the addition of an almost endless number of squares in any direction is the cone of vision. Squares constructed outside of the cone of vision will be subject to distortion in the same way as in any other method of perspective projection.

In the examples to date the measuring points have occurred in the horizon line because each of the figures used has been either in the ground plane or parallel to it, which means that the diagonals used to locate the measuring points have been parallel to the ground. The vanishing points for lines either in or parallel to the ground plane are located in the horizon line. In the example shown in Fig. 80, the side of a cube, which has been set up in perspective using a two-point construction, is used to locate a measuring point. If the diagonal of a side is drawn as shown, it can be seen that it is a line inclined to the ground plane. The diagonal drawn on the face of the cube will be in the same direction, when seen in plan, as the top and bottom edges of the cube, so that its vanishing point will be either directly above or below V.P.1. In the example shown here a measuring point (vanishing point for the diagonal and all lines parallel to it) will be below V.P.1. By extending the top and bottom lines of the appropriate side of the cube, more identical cubes can be drawn using the measuring point to draw another diagonal as each cube is completed. This can be repeated until the required number of cubes is produced. More cubes could be added in another direction if a diagonal were drawn on the other visible vertical face of the cube and extended to meet a vertical line through V.P.2. This second measuring point could then be used in the same way as the previous one to add more cubes on this side.

Another use of the measuring point is the subdivision of a surface similar to the one shown in Fig. 81. The problem illustrated

80   Drawing a series of identical cubes
with the help of a measuring point.

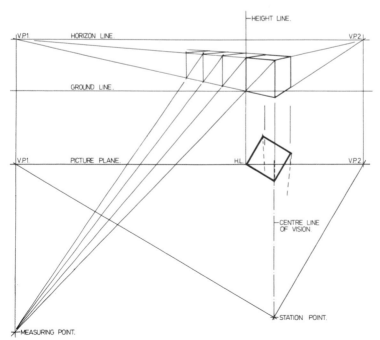

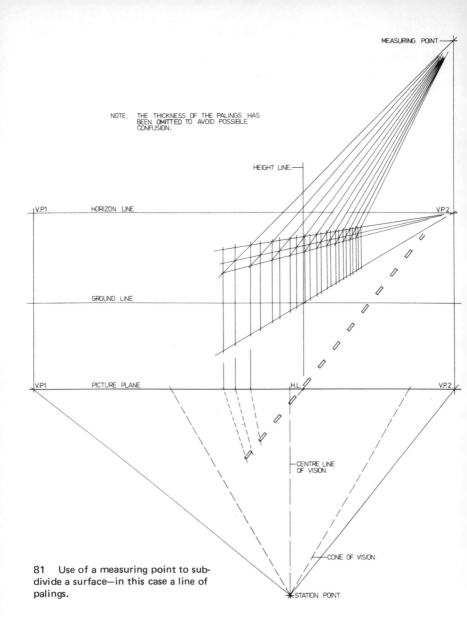

MEASURING POINT.

NOTE. THE THICKNESS OF THE PALINGS HAS
BEEN OMITTED TO AVOID POSSIBLE
CONFUSION.

HEIGHT LINE.

V.P.1.   HORIZON LINE.   V.P.2.

GROUND LINE.

V.P.1.   PICTURE PLANE.   H.L.   V.P.2.

CENTRE LINE
OF VISION.

CONE OF VISION.

STATION POINT.

81   Use of a measuring point to sub-
divide a surface—in this case a line of
palings.

here represents a paling fence with palings of one width and spaces
of another. This can be set up in perspective using the normal
method of projection, but it would be a long and laborious process. If the top and bottom lines of the palings are set up using
the normal method of perspective projection the first paling and
the first space can be located as shown. Using a convenient angle,

a line is drawn through the intersection of the top line of the fence and the top corner (next to the first space) of the second paling and continued in both directions to intersect the sides of the first paling in one direction and a vertical line drawn through V.P.2 in the other. The intersection of this line and the vertical line through V.P.2 is the measuring point, i.e. the vanishing point for this line and all others parallel to it. From the points of intersection of the line and the sides of the first paling perspective lines are drawn back to V.P.2 as shown. A line drawn from the intersection of the lower of these two perspective lines and the side of the second paling (already located) to the measuring point will locate the width of the second paling and the space between it and the third paling. This exercise can be repeated until the required length of fence has been drawn.

To sight and locate each paling by projection would require a great deal of patience together with a possible loss of accuracy as the distance between the spectator and the palings increases. Though the measuring point in this case is an arbitrary one its use is no less accurate than those which were constructed in the previous examples. The basic principle, that shapes can be repeated in perspective projection using diagonals and their vanishing points (measuring points), remains the same.

Fig. 82 shows this method used for drawing a railroad track in perspective. This is always a difficult subject because if it is not drawn accurately in the first place it can cause no end of difficulty and frustration. Because the diagonals are either in or parallel to the ground plane, the measuring point will be located in the horizon line. It is necessary first to set up enough of the plan to locate the size and relationship of the major components of the subject. In this example, using a one-point construction in the normal way, a short length of track is set up in the plan view. When the major components, i.e. the rails, sleepers and spaces between the sleepers, have been set up accurately in perspective it is possible to locate a measuring point in a convenient position in the horizon line. From this measuring point a line is drawn to the intersection of the inside base line of the rail and the nearer top edge of the sleeper nearest to the spectator. From the points of intersection of this line and the back edge of the nearest sleeper and the front edge of the second sleeper, perspective lines are drawn back to the vanishing point. It can be seen from Fig. 82 that the diagonals are drawn back to the measuring point and the sleepers and the spaces between them are located and drawn until the required length of track has been produced.

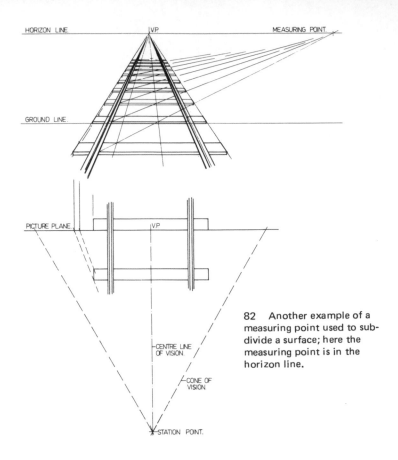

HORIZON LINE

V.P

MEASURING POINT.

GROUND LINE.

PICTURE PLANE

V.P

CENTRE LINE
OF VISION.

CONE OF
VISION.

STATION POINT.

82   Another example of a
measuring point used to sub-
divide a surface; here the
measuring point is in the
horizon line.

From the few examples shown here it can be seen that the use
of the measuring point can save a great deal of time and needless
effort without significant loss of accuracy. These examples are by
no means all of the uses to which measuring points can be applied
but once the principle is thoroughly understood it can be developed, expanded and used to solve many otherwise complex
problems.

Measuring points can also be used to set up a perspective view
of an object. This is known as the measuring point method for
setting up a perspective and the basic principle of it is shown in
Fig. 83 where, by its use, one line is located in a perspective view.
In this figure the line to be drawn in perspective is located in the
ground plane with, in this case, end *B* coinciding with the picture
plane. The station point and the picture plane are selected in the
same way as in previous constructions. To eliminate the possibility

80

of distortion the position of the station point should be checked with the cone of vision to make sure that the spectator can in fact see all of the object from the chosen station point. This step is important in any perspective drawing and is, unfortunately, often forgotten. The vanishing point for the given line is found by drawing a sight line from the station point parallel to the line to meet the picture plane. The point of intersection of this sight line and the picture plane is the plan location of the vanishing point (V.P.). The measuring point is located in the picture plane (plan) by using the vanishing point as the centre of an arc whose radius is equal to the length of the line from the station point to the vanishing point. The point where the arc intersects the picture plane is the plan location of the measuring point. The location of the horizon line is a matter of convenience; it can be located either above or below the plan construction without altering the final drawing. In Fig. 83, the horizon line is located above the plan construction and the ground line is located below the horizon line at a distance equal to the required eye-level. It is this distance which determines the height of the spectator's eye above the ground and it is therefore the relation-ship between the horizon line and the ground line which is important, not the relationship between the horizon line and the picture plane in the plan construction, as the student sometimes mistakenly assumes.

To locate the vanishing point and the measuring point on the horizon line, where they must be located because the line which is the subject of the perspective drawing is located in the ground

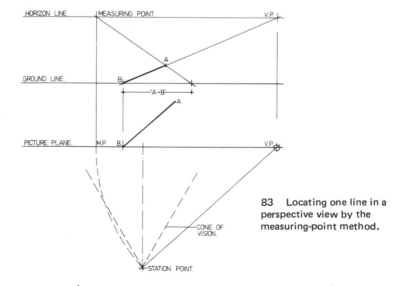

83   Locating one line in a perspective view by the measuring-point method.

plane, is a simple matter of projecting up vertically to the horizon line. If the horizon line was below the plan of the picture plane, projections would be down vertically. Because point B coincides with the picture plane and is in the ground plane it can be located in the perspective view by simple vertical projection up to the ground line. The line AB will lie in a line from point B to the vanishing point (the vanishing point was located by drawing a sight line parallel to the plan of line AB). The length of the line AB is measured in the plan and from point B in the ground line this length is measured along the ground line and marked, as shown. (This line must always be marked off on the opposite side of the line from B to V.P. to the measuring point.) By joining the measuring point and the point in the ground line marking off the length of the line AB, point A is located in the line from B to V.P. The result of this exercise is a drawing of the line AB in perspective.

Once it is possible to locate one line in a perspective view it is possible to locate any number of lines. Because a perspective drawing is essentially a line drawing and an object can be considered as simply a collection of lines, it must be possible to draw objects in perspective using the method described here for a single line. However, before proceeding with an object such as a simple rectangular prism, it is necessary to look at a few variations to the location of the single line. The first is a line which is still parallel to the ground plane but no longer situated in it. In Fig. 84, the line AB is at a height h above

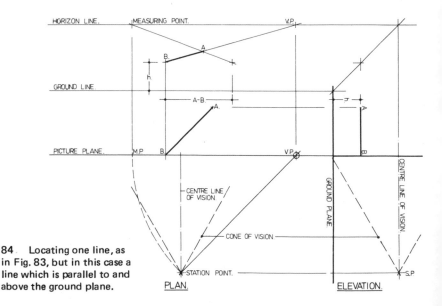

84. Locating one line, as in Fig. 83, but in this case a line which is parallel to and above the ground plane.

the ground plane but in all other respects the circumstances are the same as those in Fig. 83. For the purpose of explanation, an elevation of the plan construction is shown and, as is usual, it is at a convenient distance from the plan construction. The relationship between the eye of the spectator and the height of the line *AB* can be seen from the elevation. The location of the station point, the picture plane, the vanishing point and the measuring point is carried out in exactly the same way as in Fig. 83. In this case point *B* is located at a height *h* above the ground plane (this is measured from the elevation), therefore point *B* in the perspective view will be at a height *h* above the ground line (point *B* coincides with the picture plane). Line *AB* will be located in the line joining point *B*, at height *h* above the ground line, to the vanishing point, i.e. in the line from *B* to V.P. Because the line *AB* is at a height *h* above and parallel to the ground plane it will be necessary to locate the length of the line *AB* at a height *h* above the ground line in the perspective view. This point defining the length of the required line can then be joined to the measuring point and point *A* located in the line from point *B* to the vanishing point. The result of this exercise is a perspective drawing of the line *AB* when it is at a height *h* above the ground plane.

The second variation to the location of a single line in perspective using the measuring point method is an inclined line, i.e. a line inclined to the ground plane. If the elevation in Fig. 84 is examined it will be seen that if one end of the line *AB* were to be lifted higher than the other, the sight line parallel to it would intersect the picture plane no longer in the horizon line but either above or below it depending on which end of the line was raised. This means that the vanishing point (and the measuring point) for an inclined line would be either above or below the horizon line and located in a vertical line through the plan location of the vanishing point (and measuring point).

Fig. 85 shows the construction required when the line *AB* is inclined to the ground plane. In this example it is necessary to prepare an elevation of the plan construction to obtain the height of the vanishing point and the measuring point above or below the horizon line. Both the plan construction and the elevation are prepared in the normal way, as previously described. Point *A* is higher than point *B* which, in this case, is located in the ground plane. From the elevation the height of the vanishing point and the measuring point is measured from the horizon line. This height is then located, in this case above the horizon line, and a line drawn horizontally to enable the measuring point to be located at the same height above

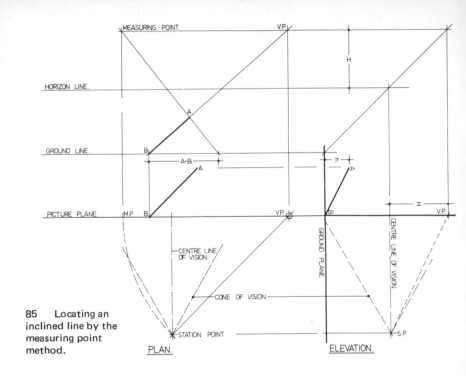

85 Locating an inclined line by the measuring point method.

PLAN.　　　　ELEVATION.

the horizon line as the vanishing point. The measuring point is located in this line by projecting up from its position in the plan view of the picture plane in the normal way. Line *AB* is drawn in the perspective view in exactly the same way as it was in the two preceding examples, the only difference being that the vanishing point and the measuring point are no longer located in the horizon line but in a horizontal line above it. From point *B* in the ground line the true length of line *AB* is measured. It should be noted that neither the plan view nor the elevation of the construction shows the true length of line *AB*, so a simple projection exercise is necessary to obtain its true length. As previously described, once the true length of the line *AB* is established, the perspective view of it can be drawn using the vanishing point and the measuring point.

In each of the previous examples of perspective drawing by the measuring point method, one end of the line to be drawn has been located in the picture plane. In the last example of single lines in perspective using this method, neither end of the line is located in the picture plane so the line must be extended to meet the picture plane at point *Ō*. Fig. 86 shows the construction required under these circumstances. The only difference between this and the previous construction shown in Fig. 83 is that the distances from point

84

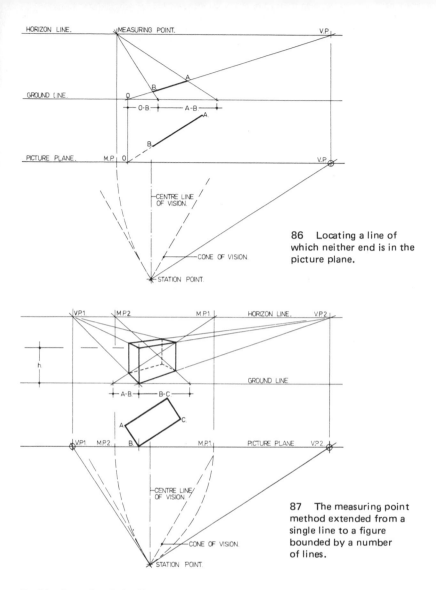

86 Locating a line of which neither end is in the picture plane.

87 The measuring point method extended from a single line to a figure bounded by a number of lines.

O of both ends of the line must be measured and located on the ground line. By joining both of the measured distances on the ground line to the measuring point the ends of line *AB* can be located.

When the basic method of constructing a perspective view using the measuring point method is understood it can be used to set up actual objects, i.e. objects consisting of a number of lines. Fig. 87 shows the method used for setting up a perspective view of a simple

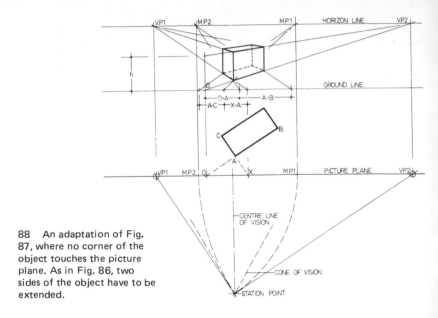

88 An adaptation of Fig. 87, where no corner of the object touches the picture plane. As in Fig. 86, two sides of the object have to be extended.

rectangular prism. Because two vanishing points are required to draw this object in perspective, it will be obvious that two measuring points will be necessary. Apart from this, the figure should be self-explanatory if the previous examples have been understood.

Fig. 88 shows the same rectangular prism as used in the preceding example but this time it has been placed at a short distance behind the picture plane. Unlike the previous example in which a corner of the prism coincided with the picture plane, in this example no corner of the prism coincides with the picture plane; this means that the appropriate sides of the prism will have to be extended to meet the picture plane in the plan construction. The vanishing points, measuring points, horizon line and ground line are located as previously explained. From the point where side *AB* is extended to meet the picture plane at point *O* in the plan construction, point *O* is located in the ground line by vertical projection. From this point *O* in the ground line the lengths *OA* and *AB* are measured and marked. The line from *O* to V.P.2 is drawn, and points *A* and *B* are located in it using the measuring point M.P.2 in the usual way. Using point *O* in the ground line as a base, the height of the rectangular prism can be established by measurement, and from this height, a line can be drawn back to V.P.2 in which the top of the side *AB* will be located. By projecting vertical lines up from points *A* and *B* in the base line of the perspective view, side *AB* can be completed. Using the extension of the side *CA* to meet the picture plane at point *X* in the plan construction, the side *CA* can be drawn in the perspective view using the same method as was used for side *AB*. Obviously it will be unnecessary to locate the height of the prism because this has already been established in the perspective view when side *AB* was drawn.

While advantages are claimed by some people for this method in comparison with others, it must be admitted that it also has a number of disadvantages, not the least of which is that it seems unnecessarily complicated. When it is remembered that for each vanishing point a measuring point is required, it will be realized that the possibility of error must be at least twice that of the method used in both this book and its companion volume *Basic Perspective*. However, it is not intended to enter into an academic discussion of the relative merits of the various methods for the construction of a perspective view of an object. Rather, the intention here is to help the student to understand and use sound knowledge of the principles of perspective projection in developing accurate methods for setting up perspective views of objects quickly and efficiently. This criticism of the measuring-point method does not extend to the use of measuring points in cases where they can be of great value in saving time without loss of accuracy, but only to the use of measuring points as the whole basis of perspective projection.

More information regarding the use of measuring points and the measuring point method of setting up perspectives is given in Chapter 9, 'Short Cuts In Perspective Drawing'.

8 Shadow projection in perspective drawing

Perspective drawing is generally only a means to an end rather than an end in itself. A perspective drawing is usually produced as a linear framework on which a rendering is based. Because light plays such an important role in what is seen, it is essential that its effect on a subject be understood so that it can be portrayed accurately when the subject is rendered. Shadow projection is seldom treated with the importance it deserves in the academic subject known as perspective, but it is nevertheless a very important part of that subject. The ability to construct accurate or, at the very least, believable shadows is one of the most important elements of rendering.

Before proceeding with the method used for constructing shadows in perspective projection it is necessary to understand a few elementary principles of light. Without light it would be impossible to see anything. An object is seen because light rays strike its surface and are reflected from that surface back to the eye of the spectator and it is only because of these reflected light rays that the spectator is able to see the object. In shadow projection it is not the reflected light ray which is of principal interest but the light ray itself. Generally speaking, there are two sources of light: the sun and the various forms of artificial light, e.g. electric light, candles, etc. Whether a light ray emanates from the sun or some form of artificial light source makes no difference to the fact that the light ray will always travel in a straight line and is incapable of changing direction unless some form of reflector is introduced. For all practical purposes light rays from the sun are considered to be parallel, unlike those from the simplest form of artificial light source which radiate from a single point. Light rays, whether from the sun or an artificial source, are incapable of penetrating solid, opaque matter. It is because of these qualities that shade and shadow exist.

To eliminate any confusion from the very beginning, it is necessary to define the difference between shade and shadow. Shade exists when a surface is turned away from the light source. Shadow exists when light rays are stopped from reaching a surface by the

intervention of another object or surface. Fig. 89 shows a post seen
in ordinary sunlight and from this view it is possible to see that the
side facing the light source is seen in light and the side facing away
from the light source is seen in shade. The line between the face
seen in light and the face seen in shade is known as the line of separation. This line of separation is of considerable importance and will
be dealt with more fully later in this chapter. Because the post stops
the light rays from reaching the ground, the area on the ground
directly behind the post will be in shadow. This shadow will start
from the base of the post, i.e. where the post meets the ground, and
finish with the first ray of light which is able to pass directly over the
top of the post. Because, in this example, only the post is capable of
stopping the light rays, the rest of the ground will be in light.

If this is related to a person standing on the ground, it will be seen
(Fig. 90a) that his shadow will start from his feet and will finish with
the topmost part of him obstructing the light rays. The only time
his shadow will not start from his feet is when his feet are no longer
in contact with the surface directly below him. An example of this
is shown in Fig.90b, where the person has jumped into the air. Because he is no longer in contact with the ground no part of him is
obstructing the light rays between his feet and the ground directly
below him, which means that his shadow will no longer start from

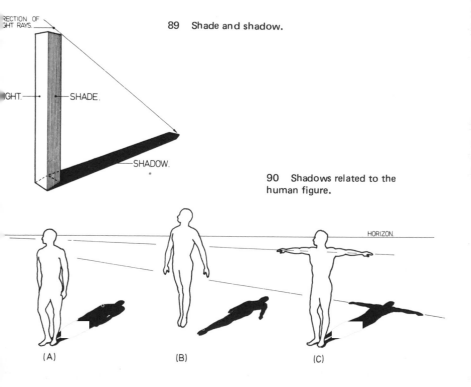

89   Shade and shadow.

90   Shadows related to the
human figure.

(A)   (B)   (C)

his feet. Nevertheless, as soon as he lands again everything will be back to normal and once again his shadow will start from his feet. This is an important fact to remember about shadows. Another is that the shadow will always fall in the direction in which the light rays travel from the light source. The third and possibly the most important of these facts to remember in shadow projection is that parallel lines cast parallel shadows. Fig.90*c* shows a person standing on the ground, i.e. at right-angles to the ground plane, with his arms raised so that they are parallel to the ground plane. The shadow cast by his outstretched arms will be parallel to his arms, i.e. the shadow cast by his arms will appear to converge to the same vanishing point as his arms.

Knowledge of these basic facts regarding shadows can save a great deal of needless effort and wasted time in setting up shadows in perspective drawing. Though these facts are possibly the most important, they are by no means all that must be considered when setting up shadows in perspective drawing. Because many of these other factors are not common to all problems, but occur only in special circumstances, they can be dealt with as they occur in the following examples.

Of the two different sources of light the first to be considered here is sunlight. Because the rays of light from the sun are for all practical purposes considered to be parallel and because they strike the ground plane obliquely, they can be treated as any other inclined lines in perspective projection. This means that because they are parallel they will converge to a common vanishing point and, because they are inclined to the ground plane, that vanishing point will be located either above or below the horizon line in the perspective view. From basic principles it is known that the vanishing point for inclined parallel lines (the light rays) will be located either directly above or below the position of the vanishing point for those lines when they are in the horizontal plane. If the sun is located in front of the spectator the vanishing point for the rays of light will be above the horizon line, as shown in Fig. 91. This means that the shadow cast by an object, in this case a person, will be towards the spectator. If, on the other hand, the sun is located behind the spectator (Fig. 92), the vanishing point for the rays of light will be below the horizon line. This means that the shadow cast by the person will be away from the spectator.

Because the shadow of an object is cast in the direction of the light rays and extends from the base of the object (if the base of the object is located in the ground plane) to the shadow point of the

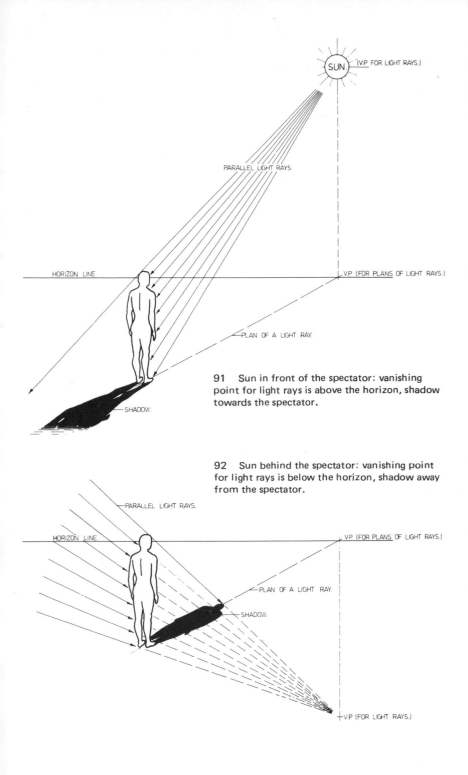

SUN. (V.P. FOR LIGHT RAYS.)

PARALLEL LIGHT RAYS.

HORIZON LINE

V.P. (FOR PLANS OF LIGHT RAYS.)

PLAN OF A LIGHT RAY.

91 Sun in front of the spectator: vanishing point for light rays is above the horizon, shadow towards the spectator.

SHADOW.

92 Sun behind the spectator: vanishing point for light rays is below the horizon, shadow away from the spectator.

PARALLEL LIGHT RAYS.

HORIZON LINE.

V.P. (FOR PLANS OF LIGHT RAYS.)

PLAN OF A LIGHT RAY.

SHADOW.

V.P. (FOR LIGHT RAYS.)

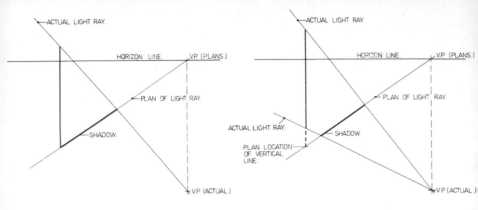

93   The shadow of a simple vertical line.

94   The shadow of a vertical line of which the lower end stands above the ground plane.

top of that object, it is possible to produce the shadow of a simple vertical line in a perspective view, as in Fig. 93. The line is shown at right-angles to the ground plane, and the direction of the light rays appears on the ground plane in the form of a line which represents a plan view of the actual ray of light. This plan of the light ray starts from the base of the vertical line. Both ends of the vertical line will coincide when it is viewed in plan, which means that the plan of the light ray drawn is the plan of that light ray which passes through the top of the vertical line. Therefore the shadow of the top of the vertical line will be located at the intersection of the plan of the light ray and the actual light ray passing through the top of the vertical line. If this principle is applied to a line which is still vertical but does not have one end located in the ground plane, as shown in Fig. 94, it will be seen that again both ends of the line would coincide in the plan view; therefore, the plans of the light rays through the top and the bottom of the line and its plan position in the ground plane would coincide in the plan view. This means that in the view shown in Fig. 94 it is necessary to locate the plan position of the vertical line in the ground plane and the plan view of the rays of light (the ones which pass through the top and the bottom of the vertical line which will coincide in the plan view) drawn from it in the direction of the light rays. The shadow position of the top of the vertical line is located in the plan of the light ray by drawing the actual light ray through the top of the vertical line to intersect the plan line. The intersection of the actual light ray and the plan of the light ray will be the shadow point of the top of the vertical line. The shadow point of the bottom of the vertical line is located in the plan of the light

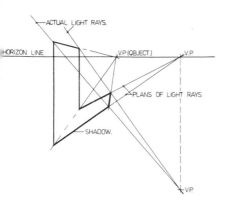

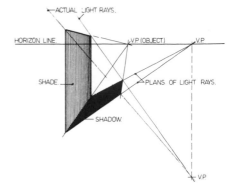

95 Shadows of two vertical lines and a cross-bar.

96 Fig. 95 converted into a vertical plane.

ray by drawing the actual light ray through the bottom of the vertical line to intersect the plan of the light ray. The intersection of the actual light ray and its plan will be the shadow point of the bottom of the vertical line. The part of the plan of the ray of light between these two points will be the shadow cast by the vertical line.

The third of these simple explanations concerns two vertical lines set apart with a horizontal line joining their tops. Fig. 95 shows the plan of the light ray for each vertical line drawn from their intersections with the ground plane. The shadow points of the tops of each line are located on these plan lines by drawing the actual light rays through the tops of these lines to meet the plans of the light rays, as previously described. The line joining the tops of the vertical lines is horizontal, i.e. parallel to the ground plane. This means that the shadow of this line joining the tops of the vertical lines will also be parallel to the ground plane.

Fig. 96 shows a vertical opaque plane which is produced by using the same vertical lines as in Fig. 95 but in this case joined by horizontal lines at the bottom as well as the top. The shadows of the lines surrounding the vertical plane are located in exactly the same way as for the lines in Fig. 95. In this example the lines will stop the rays of light from reaching the ground but also, because the lines enclose an opaque surface, no light ray will be able to reach the ground within an area bounded by these lines. Consequently the area between the shadows of these lines will be seen in shadow. It should be remembered that the surface of the vertical plane facing away from the light source will be in shade.

From the examples shown here it can be seen by examination,

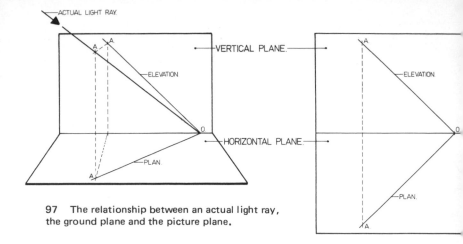

97 The relationship between an actual light ray,
the ground plane and the picture plane.

particularly of Figs. 95 and 96, that the shadows of the objects can
be completed by simple observation and logic: if each object is
treated as a combination of simple lines, shadows need be neither
difficult nor time-consuming.

From the foregoing it should be obvious that before shadows can
be constructed in a perspective projection the direction of the light
rays and their angle of inclination to the ground plane must be
known. Because a perspective projection is carried out in two dimensions, not three which would be necessary to take advantage of the
conditions shown in Fig. 97, it is necessary to locate a plan view and
an elevation of the actual light ray so that when the vertical plane is
'laid down flat', as shown, it is possible to use these views for the
perspective construction. While the angle between the plan of the
light ray and the picture plane is the true angle, the angle of inclination, i.e. the angle the inclined light rays make with the ground plane,
shown in this view, is not. For the angle of inclination to be seen as a
true angle it would have to be seen parallel to the vertical plane,
therefore in this view it will appear distorted, i.e. larger than it will
be in fact. In perspective projection it is necessary to produce a true
elevation of the actual light ray so that the true angle the light ray
makes with the ground plane can be used. The method for obtaining
this true inclination of the actual light ray is shown in Fig. 98, where
the angle formed by the actual light ray and the ground plane is
swung through an arc which results in the true angle being located
on the picture plane without distortion. When the vertical plane is
'laid down flat' it can be seen that the true angle of inclination of
the light ray is much smaller than the angle shown in Fig. 97. To
relate this to perspective projection the angle which the plan of the

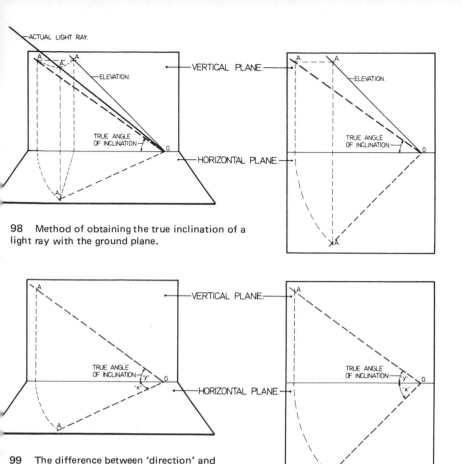

98 Method of obtaining the true inclination of a light ray with the ground plane.

99 The difference between 'direction' and 'inclination'.

light ray makes with the picture plane is known as the *direction* of the light ray (angle *x*) and the true inclination of the light ray is known as the *inclination* (angle *y*). These angles are shown and identified in Fig. 99 to avoid any confusion.

For the purpose of explaining the method used for the construction of shadows in perspective projection a simple rectangular prism has been set up using a two-point construction (Fig. 100). When the perspective view of the object is completed, it is necessary to decide on the location of the light source, i.e. the direction (angle *x*) and the inclination (angle *y*) of the light rays. Because the light rays are parallel and their plan lines are parallel it is necessary to locate vanishing points for each of them.

These vanishing points are located in three main steps (Fig. 101):

95

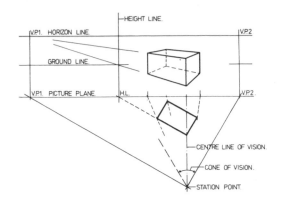

100   Rectangular prism in perspective, ready for construction of shadows.

Step 1. Using the station point as the starting point, a sight line parallel to the plan view of the light ray is drawn to meet the picture plane (plan) at the angle x. The intersection of this sight line and the picture plane (plan) is the plan location of the vanishing points (V. 1) for both the actual light rays and their plans. Because the plans of the light rays will occur in a horizontal plane (the ground plane or planes parallel to it), the vanishing point for these plan lines will be located in the horizon line. This means that V. 1, which was located in the picture plane (plan), is projected up vertically in the normal way to locate it in the horizon line. It is known that the vanishing point for the actual light rays, which are simply inclined lines, will be located either directly above or below the vanishing point for their plans (V.1). This means that the vanishing point for the actual light rays will be located somewhere in the vertical line drawn through V.1.

Step 2. Before locating the vanishing point for the actual light rays it is necessary to locate the true angle y (the angle the light ray makes with the ground plane) on the picture plane. The sight line used to locate V.1 in Step 1 is a plan line drawn parallel to the light ray; therefore if this sight line (which is in fact a plan view of a sight line drawn parallel to the actual light ray) is swung through an arc with centre V.1 and radius V.1 to S.P. it is possible to obtain the true angle of inclination of the light ray (angle y) on the picture plane. Point O is located in the picture plane at the point where the arc intersects it. Point O is then located in the horizon line (because a sight line is used and the horizon line coincides with the eye-level) by vertical projection in the normal way. Because point O in the horizon line is the equivalent of the 'eye-position' and the vertical line through V.1 is the equivalent of an end elevation of the picture plane, a sight line could be

96

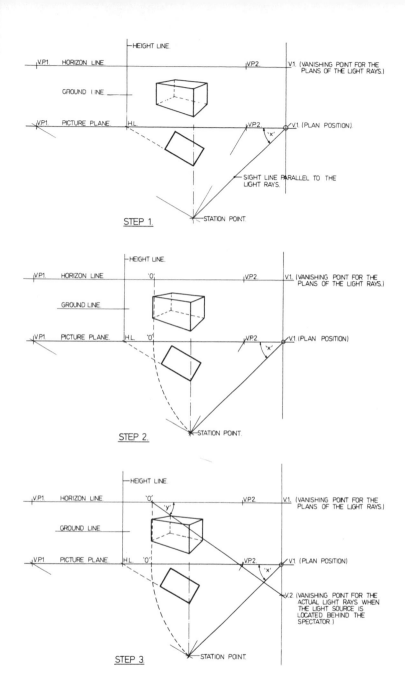

101 Locating the vanishing points of the light rays, when the light is coming from behind the spectator.

drawn from the 'eye-position' (point *O*) parallel to the true angle of inclination of the light ray (andle *y*) to meet the vertical line through V.1. (The equivalent of the end elevation of the picture plane.) This intersection of the sight line and the picture plane, i.e. the line drawn from point *O* at angle *y* to the horizon line to meet the vertical line through V.1, will be the vanishing point for the actual light rays.

Step 3. To locate the vanishing point for the actual light rays when the light source is located behind the spectator (which means that it will be located below the horizon line, as previously described), it is necessary to draw a line from point *O* (in the horizon line) at the angle *y* (below the horizon line) to meet the vertical line drawn through V.1. The point V.2, located at the intersection of these two lines, is the vanishing point for the actual light rays when the light source is located behind the spectator.

If the light source is located in front of the spectator the three steps remain basically the same except that the angle *y* in Step 3 is located above the horizon line, as shown in Fig. 102, in which V.3, above the horizon line, represents the vanishing point for the actual light rays. The sun (the light source) can be in only one place at a time, therefore either V.2 (behind the spectator) or V.3 (in front of the spectator) will be required in any perspective drawing but never both in the same drawing even though V.1 is common to both constructions. Needless to say, if the light source were located on the right of the spectator, instead of on his left as shown in Figs. 101 and 102, it would be necessary to locate V.1 on the other side of the

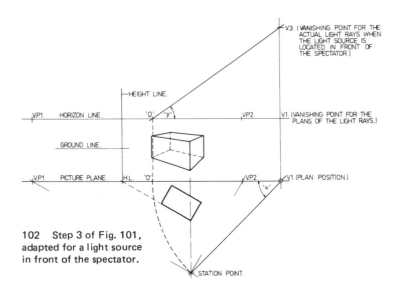

98

102   Step 3 of Fig. 101, adapted for a light source in front of the spectator.

construction using exactly the same method as for the examples shown.

An important factor is that the method shown here gives the student complete freedom in his choice of the direction and inclination of the light source. However, if the subject of his perspective drawing is a building or any other object which has a fixed aspect, this aspect can easily be related to the plan under projection because the angle the sun makes with both the picture plane and the ground plane can be calculated for any time of the day, for any month of the year, for any location in the world. Because this can be done, using this method, exact shadows can be cast for any set of realistic conditions anywhere in the world. To help in this and other areas relating to sun control, tables of sun angles are available for most of the major cities of the world or, at the very least, for the various latitudes of the world. However, it is not intended to pursue this aspect of shadow projection here because once the basic method is understood, whether actual angles or arbitrary ones are used, the method for carrying out the construction of shadows in perspective projection will be the same. Further information on a short-cut method of locating the vanishing points required in shadow projection is given in the next chapter (p. 131).

Once the construction required for setting up shadows in perspective has been completed, it is possible to locate and draw the shadows of the object forming the subject of the exercise. Fig. 103 shows four examples of objects and their shadows when the light source is behind the spectator (V.2 — will be below the horizon line). The construction used to locate the vanishing point for the plans of the light rays (V.1) and the vanishing point for the actual light rays (V.2) is shown for the first of the four examples only (Fig.103a) and would be exactly the same for the other three. Using these two vanishing points (V.1 and V.2), it is possible to construct the correct shadows of the object under these specific conditions.

In the example shown in Fig.103a, it is first necessary, after setting up the vanishing points, to select a starting point for the actual construction of the shadow of the object. In this example the vertical line *AB* is chosen as the starting point. From the point of intersection of this line and the ground plane (point *B*) a line representing the plan of the light ray passing through the top of the vertical line is drawn in perspective, i.e. back to V.1. The actual light ray is then drawn through the top of the vertical line (point *A*) back to V.2. The point of intersection of these two lines is the

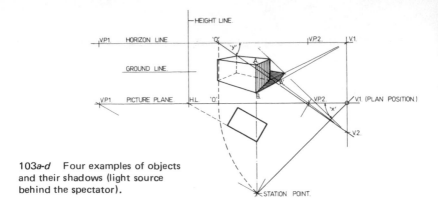

HEIGHT LINE

V.P.1.   HORIZON LINE   'O'   V.P.2.   V.1

GROUND LINE

V.P.1   PICTURE PLANE   H.L   'O'   V.P.2   V.1. (PLAN POSITION.)

V.2.

STATION POINT.

103*a-d*   Four examples of objects and their shadows (light source behind the spectator).

shadow of point *A* in the perspective view. This means that the line on the ground plane between point *B* (the base of the vertical line) and point *A* (the top of the vertical line) must represent, in the perspective view, the shadow of the vertical line *AB*. The other vertical 'edges' of the rectangular prism can have their shadows projected in the same way. If the object is examined it will be seen that these verticals form the vertical edges of solid planes which have top and bottom edges also. The top edges of these planes can be dealt with in either one of two ways. The first uses the fact that the top of the line *AB* is joined to the top of the opposite vertical edge of the plane by a straight line; therefore, the shadows of the verticals will be joined by the shadow of this straight line. In this way, the shadows of each of the planes forming the rectangular prism can be located and drawn in the perspective view.

On the other hand, it is known that parallel lines cast parallel shadows, and, because these straight lines joining the tops of the vertical lines of the object are parallel to the ground plane, the shadows cast by them will be parallel, i.e. they will be drawn using the same vanishing point as the lines themselves. It will be seen that the answer in both cases will be exactly the same; only the reasoning differs. The 'parallel line casting a parallel shadow' theory is usually preferred because it can save a great deal of time and confusion in many cases.

Once the method of actually drawing shadows in perspective projection is understood, it is a simple matter to apply it to any object, no matter how complex it might be. Basically, shadow projection is the ability to cast the shadow of a vertical line or 'stick' and repeat the example the required number of times, joining the tops and bottoms of these vertical lines where necessary and remembering that parallel lines cast parallel shadows.

Fig. 103*b* shows an example of an object, again a simple rectangular prism, which in this case is suspended above the ground plane. Before the shadow can be constructed in this example, it is necessary to locate the positions of the four corners of the object in the ground plane so that the plans of the light rays can be drawn. Once the plan positions of the corners of the object have been located, the shadow is constructed by locating the intersections of the plan lines (drawn back to V.1) and the actual light rays (drawn back to V.2) through the corners of the object.

Fig.103*c* shows the same rectangular prism, in the same position as for Fig. 103*a*, with a post located so that the shadow of the post will be cast across it. The shadow of the prism is exactly the same as it was in Fig. 103*a* and is constructed in exactly the same way. The post is a little more complicated because its shadow falls not only on the ground plane but also on the surface of the rectangular prism. Therefore, it will be necessary to project the plan of the light ray on the ground plane first. This is done by using V.1 in the normal way together with the actual light ray which is drawn through the top of the post using V.2. Because the rectangular prism is opaque, the shadow of the post will not be able to penetrate the surface of the prism; therefore it must be seen on the surface of the prism. If the shadow line from the base of the post is followed, it will be seen that it will run across the ground to the base of the verti-

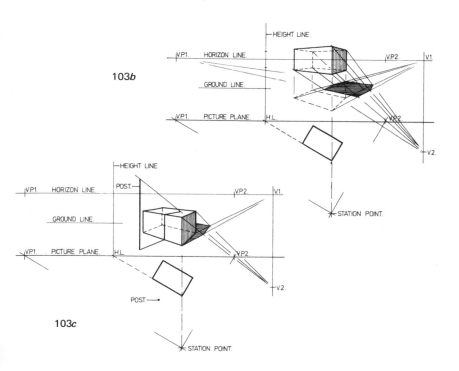

103*b*

103*c*

cal plane forming the side of the prism facing the spectator. Because the post is parallel to that vertical side of the prism, its shadow will be parallel to the post, which means that it will run vertically up the surface of the prism. When the shadow of the post reaches the top of the vertical face of the prism, it will again encounter a horizontal plane (the top surface of the rectangular prism) which is parallel to the ground plane. This means that the shadow will continue across this horizontal plane in the same direction as it was travelling on the ground plane (using V.1), until it meets the actual light ray which will locate the shadow point of the top of the post. If the progress of a shadow is followed in a drawing in this way, the more obvious mistakes can be eliminated and, by applying a little common sense, shadows can be drawn simply and quickly and, above all, accurately.

In the final example in this figure, the rectangular prism has had a part cut out so that a shadow is cast by a part of the object on its own surface. Fig. 103*d* shows that the plan positions of the corners of the object not in contact with the ground plane must first be located in the ground plane. Once this is done, the plans of the light rays can be drawn (using V.1) on the ground plane — at least, they can be drawn as far as they go before they meet the vertical plane of the object. When they reach this vertical plane they will run up the vertical surface (vertically because parallel lines cast parallel shadows). The actual light rays are drawn through the appropriate corners of the object (using V.2) and where the actual light rays intersect the plans of the light rays (which in this case are running up the vertical face of the object) the shape of the shadow cast by the projection on the vertical surface of the object can be drawn. The shadow which the main object casts on the ground plane is constructed in the same way as already described for the other three examples in this figure.

If the four examples shown in Fig. 103 are understood, any shadows can be cast when the light source is behind the spectator

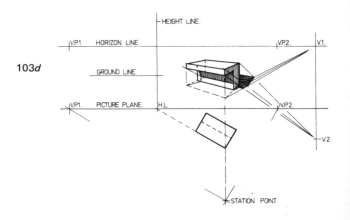

103*d*

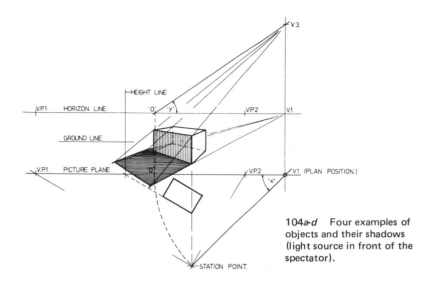

104*a-d* Four examples of objects and their shadows (light source in front of the spectator).

whatever the complexity of the shape of the object observed. The examples shown in Fig. 103 concentrate on the construction of the shadows cast by the objects and no mention is made of the surfaces which will be seen in shade. Because shade occurs when a face of the object is turned away from the light source no construction is necessary. Instead shade is located by common-sense, logical observation which is helped considerably by locating the line of separation, i.e. the line separating the faces of the object seen 'in light' and those seen 'in shade'. In the four examples in Fig. 103, the lines of separation should be obvious and most can be learned about the line of separation by observation at this stage.

Fig. 104 also consists of four examples of shadows cast by a simple object but in this case they are set up using a light source which is located in front of the spectator. This means that the vanishing point for the actual light rays will be located above the horizon line (V.3) Using the same rectangular prism and the same two-point construction as used in Fig. 103, a perspective view of the prism is set up. Fig. 104*a* shows the construction used for locating V.1 (the vanishing point for the plans of the light rays) and V.3 (the vanishing point for the actual rays when the light source is in front of the spectator). The method for carrying out this construction is exactly the same as the one used to locate V.2 in Fig.103*a* except that angle *y* is set out above the horizon line instead of below it. Because the construction will be the same for all four examples in this figure it has been omitted from the other three. The shadow is constructed by drawing the plans of the light rays using V.1 and the actual light

103

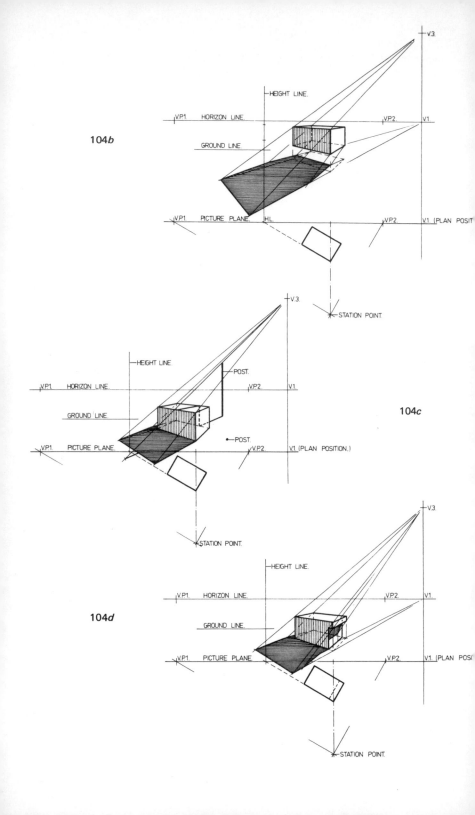

104b

V.3.

HEIGHT LINE.

V.P.1.   HORIZON LINE.   V.P.2.   V.1.

GROUND LINE.

V.P.1.   PICTURE PLANE.   H.L.   V.P.2.   V.1. (PLAN POSIT

STATION POINT.

V.3.

HEIGHT LINE.

POST.

V.P.1.   HORIZON LINE.   V.P.2.   V.1.

GROUND LINE.

104c

V.P.1.   PICTURE PLANE.   POST.   V.P.2.   V.1. (PLAN POSITION.)

STATION POINT.

V.3.

HEIGHT LINE.

V.P.1.   HORIZON LINE.   V.P.2.   V.1.

104d

GROUND LINE.

V.P.1.   PICTURE PLANE.   V.P.2.   V.1. (PLAN POSI

STATION POINT.

rays using V.3. The intersections of these lines are then joined up using the 'parallel lines casting parallel shadows' theory and in this way the shadow of the rectangular prism is drawn in the perspective view. In this example, the shadow of the prism will be in front of the object, which is consistent with a light source located in front of the spectator. (Note the surface of the prism which, in this case, will be in shade.)

Fig. 104*b* shows another example of a shadow cast by using a light source located in front of the spectator. In this example the rectangular prism is suspended above the ground plane. As was the case in Fig. 103*b*, it is necessary to locate the four corners of the rectangular prism in the ground plane. The plans of the light rays are then drawn using V.1 and the actual light rays are drawn using V.3. By joining up the points of intersection of these lines, the shadow of the suspended rectangular prism is drawn. Again the same face will be seen in shade as was the case in Fig. 104*a*.

Fig.104*c* shows a post located in relation to the rectangular prism so that its shadow will fall across the prism and terminate on the ground beyond it. The shadow cast by the prism will be the same as shown in Fig.104*a* and the same face will be in shade. The post will cast a shadow which will start from its base and proceed across the ground plane until it meets the vertical face of the rectangular prism (not seen by the spectator) where it will run up this vertical plane (vertically) until it reaches the top surface, which is horizontal (parallel to the ground plane). It will travel across this surface in the same direction as it was travelling on the ground plane, i.e. back to V.1. If the actual light ray is drawn from V.3 through the top of the post it will intersect the plan of the light ray at a point beyond the shadow of the prism; therefore the plan of the light ray will have to continue on the ground (as a continuation of the plan line established from the base of the post) until it intersects the actual light ray.

Fig.104*d* shows a rectangular prism with a part cut out so that the part left will cast a shadow on the vertical surface of the remaining part of the prism. The plan positions of the part casting the shadow must first be located on the ground plane. Once this has been done, the plans of the light rays can be drawn (using V.1) on the ground plane, until they meet the vertical surface of the object. In this example only one of these plan lines will meet the base of the vertical face, which means that it will run up the vertical surface (vertically) until it meets the appropriate actual light ray (drawn using V.3). In this way the shadow of the projection can be drawn on the vertical surface of the object. The fact that parallel lines cast parallel shadows is used to advantage in this exercise. The shadow of the object itself is cast on the ground plane in the normal way. Finally the area seen in shade can again be determined by observation.

The foregoing examples of shadow projection have been based on two-point perspective constructions but the method of construction shown is equally suited to the other types of perspective constructions such as one-point and three-point. The first of these to be dealt with here is the one-point construction. For simplicity of explanation a rectangular prism is again used. The prism is set up using the normal method, described previously (Fig.105). Assuming again that the direction of the light rays make an angle x with the picture plane and an angle y with the ground plane, the construction is identical to that described in Fig.101. Again, if the light source is located behind the spectator the angle y (the angle of inclination) is set out below the horizon line as shown. If the light source is located in front of the spectator the angle y will be set out above the horizon line as shown in Fig.106. From this point on, the shadow of the prism is located in exactly the same way as the ones under the same conditions in the two-point constructions, i.e. the shadow of the prism in Fig.105 will be behind the object as seen by the spectator, and the shadow of the prism in Fig.106 will be in front of the prism as seen by the spectator.

The third and last type of perspective construction to be dealt with here is the three-point construction. A three-point construction is required when an object is placed in relationship to a spectator so that none of its edges is either horizontal or vertical, e.g. when the object is made up of parallel sides which are at right angles to each other such as a rectangular prism. In other words, each set of parallel

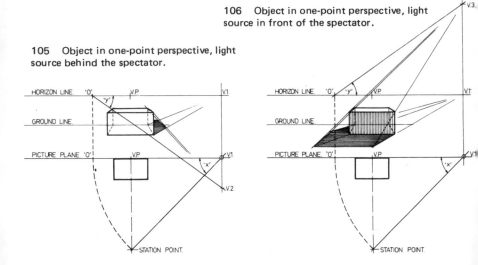

106   Object in one-point perspective, light source in front of the spectator.

105   Object in one-point perspective, light source behind the spectator.

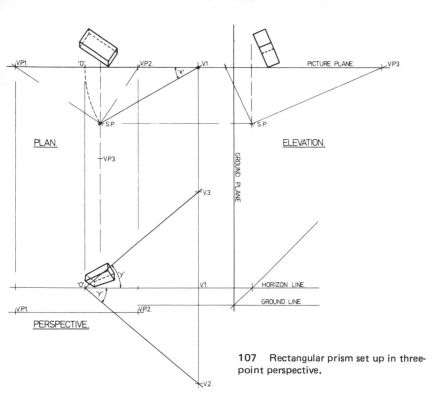

PLAN.

ELEVATION.

PERSPECTIVE.

107 Rectangular prism set up in three-point perspective.

lines forming the shape of the object is inclined to both the picture plane and the ground plane. Fig. 107 shows a rectangular prism set up using a three-point perspective construction. The preparation of the special plan and other construction lines have been omitted from this diagram to avoid unnecessary confusion but the method used was exactly the same as previously described. From this figure it can be seen that the method used for locating the vanishing points for the plans of the light rays (V.1) and the vanishing points for the actual light rays (V.2 or V.3) is identical to the one used for both one-point and two-point constructions. Both V.2 and V.3 have been shown located but it will be realized that one or the other, never both, will be required in any one drawing.

To avoid confusion at such a small scale the actual construction of the shadow has not been shown in this example but, because the prism is suspended above the gound plane, it would be necessary to locate a plan (in perspective) of the prism on the ground plane so that the plans of the light rays could be located in the normal way. The shadow cast by the suspended prism could then be completed by drawing the actual light rays using either V.2 or V.3, depending on

107

the location of the light source, and the appropriate vanishing points. Because the method of locating the vanishing points for the plans of the light rays and for the actual light rays are identical for each of the the three types of perspective construction, and the method for constructing the shadows is also identical, it is not considered necessary to show individual examples of each type of construction for the various shapes dealt with in the remainder of this section.

Fig.108 shows a group of solid objects one of which has an inclined plane set up in perspective in which one-point and two-point constructions are included. The construction lines for the perspective constructions and the location of the vanishing points for the plans of the light rays and for the actual light rays have been omitted to avoid confusion, but it is obvious that the previously-described methods have been used to produce the diagram. Apart from the fact that the shadow of the taller prism falls on the other one, little need be added to the explanations already given for constructing the shadows of these objects. As in the examples where the shadow of the post fell on the prism described previously, if the progress of the shadow is followed carefully, the problem of the shadow of one object falling on another object should not disconcert the student. (Again the areas seen in shade, together with the line of separation

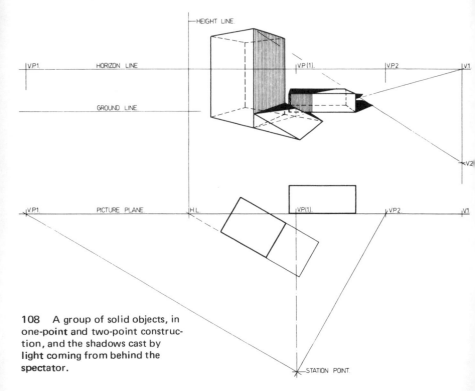

108   A group of solid objects, in one-point and two-point construction, and the shadows cast by light coming from behind the spectator.

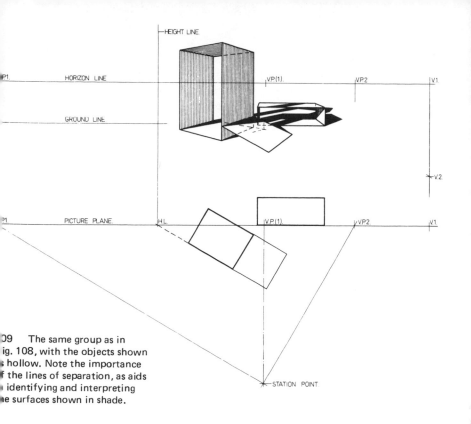

09   The same group as in
ig. 108, with the objects shown
hollow. Note the importance
f the lines of separation, as aids
identifying and interpreting
e surfaces shown in shade.

for each object, are worth noting.) The shadow cast on the inclined
plane is simply a matter of drawing the plan of the light ray on the
ground plane to meet the plan of the inclined line. From the point
of intersection of these two plan lines a vertical projection is made
to meet the inclined line. From this point on the inclined line, the
shadow line can be drawn back to the line of separation of the
prism casting the shadow. The construction used here to locate the
shadow on an inclined plane is shown and described more fully in
Fig. 110.

To avoid any confusion, the shadows cast on horizontal and
inclined planes are shown in solid black in Figs. 108 through to
115.

Fig. 109 is somewhat similar to the previous example but with
one significant difference: the objects in this example are all hollow.
This means that the number of surfaces seen by the spectator is
considerably increased, with the result that not only the shadows
on the ground plane, but also those which are cast on the vertical

surfaces, are important. In this example the lines of separation
become very important because it is from them that those surfaces
which will be seen in shade can be correctly identified and shown.
The actual construction of the shadows on this example can be
carried out in exactly the same way as described for the previous
one.

In all the previous examples where a line or plane is located
above the ground plane, it is necessary to locate the plans of these
lines or planes on the ground plane. This means that it is necessary,
in the example shown in Fig. 110, to locate the plans of the inclined
lines (the sides of the inclined plane). Once these plan lines have
been located the construction is straightforward. The shadow cast
by the vertical plane on the ground is located by drawing the plans
of the light rays from the bases of the two vertical edges of the plane
and the actual light rays through the tops of these vertical edges. The
shadow cast by the inclined plane on the ground plane is located by
drawing an actual light ray through the intersection of the inclined
plane and the vertical plane (on the side which will cast the shadow
on the ground plane). Where this light ray meets the shadow of the
vertical edge of the vertical plane is the required shadow point. The
shadow of the inclined plane is located by joining the shadow
point of the intersection of the two edges of the planes to the intersection of the appropriate edge of the inclined plane and the ground
plane. The shadow of the vertical plane cast on the inclined plane
is located by projecting up from the intersection of the shadow line

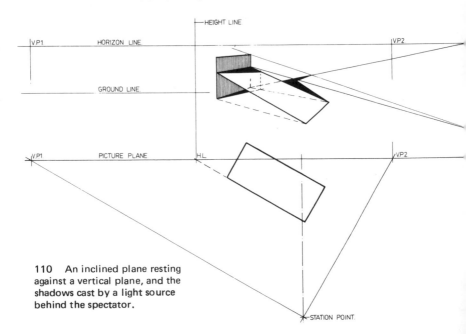

110 An inclined plane resting
against a vertical plane, and the
shadows cast by a light source
behind the spectator.

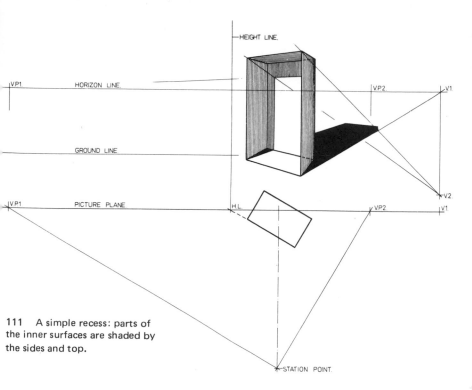

V.P1.   HORIZON LINE.   VP2   V1

GROUND LINE

V.P1   PICTURE PLANE   H.L.   VP2   V1

V2

STATION POINT.

111   A simple recess: parts of
the inner surfaces are shaded by
the sides and top.

of the edge of the vertical plane and the plan of the inclined line
which represents the edge of the inclined plane. The point where
this vertical projection meets the edge of the inclined plane is then
joined to the point of intersection of the opposite inclined edge of
the inclined plane and the vertical plane casting the shadow. Finally,
as with the previous two examples, the surfaces seen in shade are
identified and indicated.

Fig. 111 shows a simple recess set up in two-point perspective,
with a light source located so that shadows of a side and the top
will be cast on the back surface of the recess. Using V.1, the plan of
the light ray is drawn from the base of the front edge of the vertical
side of the recess to meet the base of the back surface of the recess
where it will proceed vertically up the vertical surface (parallel lines
cast parallel shadows) until it meets the actual light ray through the
top of the vertical edge. Because parallel lines cast parallel shadows,
the shadow cast by the top of the recess can be drawn from the
shadow point of the top of the vertical side, using V.P.1. Finally,
the shadow of the object is cast on the ground plane in the normal
way.

Fig. 112 shows another recess: in this case the top is no longer

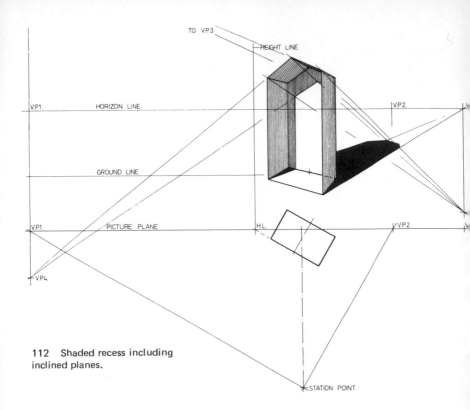

TO V.P.3

HEIGHT LINE

V.P.1

HORIZON LINE

V.P.2

GROUND LINE

V.P.1

PICTURE PLANE

H.L.

V.P.2

V.P.4

112 Shaded recess including inclined planes.

STATION POINT.

horizontal but is made up of two inclined planes of equal length. Because the planes forming the top of this recess are inclined planes it will be necessary to locate V.P.3 and V.P.4 (vanishing points for the inclined lines) when setting up the object in perspective projection. The shadow of the vertical side is cast on the back surface in exactly the same way as for the preceding example. Because parallel lines cast parallel shadows, the shadow of the inclined lines forming the edges of the inclined planes of the top of the recess are drawn using V.P.3 and V.P.4. The shadow of the object is cast on the ground plane in the usual way.

Fig.113 shows a hollow triangular-shaped object suspended above the ground. Once the plan of the object is located on the ground plane in the perspective view, the shadow can be located using V.1 and V.2 in the normal way. The side seen in shade is straightforward but, because the object is hollow, it will be possible to see part of the shadow cast by one side on another. There are a number of ways in which this shadow can be located but perhaps the simplest way is to work back from the shadow cast by the object on the ground. If the shadows of the two sides under consideration are located, it will be seen that it is a fairly simple matter to locate the intersection of the shadow of the top edge of the 'front' surface and the shadow of the bottom edge of the 'back' surface. By using V.2 this point of intersection can be located on the bottom edge of the 'back' surface of the actual object. This point is then joined to the intersection of the top edges of the two surfaces under consideration. This sounds a little complicated but if the construction is followed in the example shown in Fig.113 it will be seen that it is simply using the principles in reverse. If the principles of shadow projection in perspective have been thoroughly understood the student should have little trouble with this type of subject. Similarly circles, cylinders and spheres should be readily understood.

Fig.114 shows a disk suspended above the ground plane, set up with a one-point perspective construction. The vanishing points for the plans of the light rays (V.1) and the actual light rays (V.2) are located as previously described. The plan of the disk is located in the ground plane in the usual way. Because it is necessary to use the perspective view of the square surrounding the circle, together with its diagonals and axes, to locate the ellipse representing the perspective view of the circle, it is also necessary to use the 'shadow' of this square to locate the shadow of the disk contained within it. It should be remembered that because parallel lines cast parallel shadows, a disk located parallel to the ground plane will cast a circular shadow,

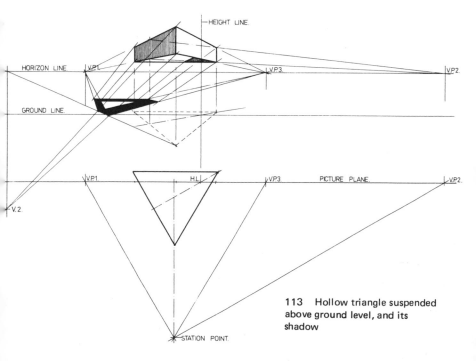

113 Hollow triangle suspended above ground level, and its shadow

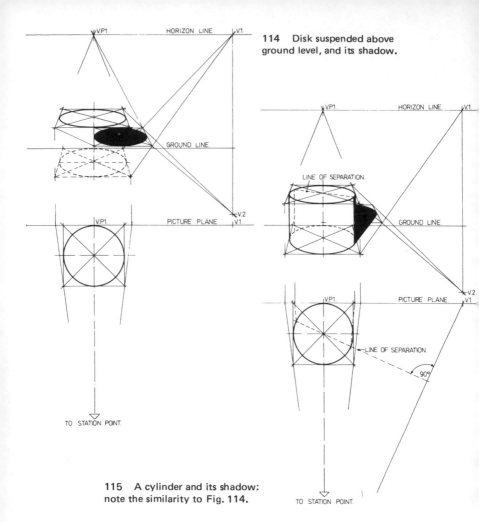

114 Disk suspended above ground level, and its shadow.

115 A cylinder and its shadow; note the similarity to Fig. 114.

and because the light rays from the sun are parallel, this shadow will be exactly the same size as the disk casting it. The 'shadow' of the square seen in the perspective view is located in the usual way using V.1 and V.2 together with its 'vertical' and 'horizontal' axes and diagonals. The points of intersection of the ellipse and these diagonals and axes are located in the shadow, again using V.1 and V.2. When the shadow points of the intersections of the ellipse and the diagonals and the axes are joined up they will result in the shadow shape of the disk seen in perspective.

The similarity between a disk suspended above the ground plane and a cylinder can be seen by examining Fig.115. The shadow of the top of the cylinder is located in exactly the same way as for the

disk in Fig.114. The bottom of the cylinder coincides with the
ground plane so it is unnecessary to construct a shadow for the
bottom because the base and its shadow coincide. It is necessary
to locate the line of separation for the cylinder so that the part of
the surface of the cylinder which will be seen in shade can be located
accurately and shown. This is done by drawing a line through the
centre of the circle in plan at right angles to the light rays. The
points where this line of separation meets the circumference of
the circle representing the plan view of the cylinder are then projected up in the normal way and are located in the perspective view.
Once the line of separation is located on the surface of the cylinder
the points of intersection of the line of separation and the ellipses
forming the ends of the cylinder can be used to locate the shadow of
the side (vertical) of the cylinder.

To this stage the disks have been located parallel to the ground
plane and, as can be seen from the two preceding examples, they
are fairly simple to deal with when shadows are required in perspective projection. The problem is simply one of drawing the
'shadow' of a square seen in perspective. If this approach is used
for a disk located at right-angles to the ground plane, as shown in
Fig.116, it will be seen that the problem is again simply a matter of
drawing the 'shadow' of a square together with its axes and diagonals.
Using V.1 and V.2, the shadows of the points of intersection between
the ellipse and the diagonals and the axes can be located in the shadow where they can be joined up to result in the shadow of the disk
on the ground plane.

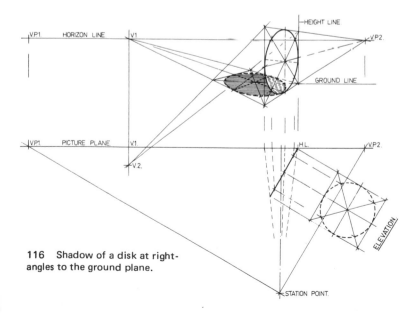

116 Shadow of a disk at right-
angles to the ground plane.

Once the shadow of a disk has been mastered in both the horizontal and vertical planes, it can easily be adapted to many objects. Its adaption to the cylinder, as shown in Fig.115, was little more than a matter of being able to draw the shadow of a disk suspended above the ground plane. The adaptation of the ability to draw the shadow of a disk to other shapes, such as the cone, should be obvious; therefore it is not intended further to pursue the matter of shadows of disks as cast by sunlight.

Fig.117 shows a sphere set up in perspective as previously described in Figs. 55 and 56. The vanishing points for the plans of the light rays (V.1) and for the actual light rays (V.2) are located in the normal way, angle x representing the direction of the light rays and angle y their inclination. The method of locating and drawing the shadow cast by a sphere is as follows:

Step 1. The major axis of the line of separation (which will appear as an ellipse in the plan view) is located in plan view of the sphere, at right-angles to the plan view of the light ray.

Step 2. At this state is is necessary to prepare an elevation of the sphere parallel to the direction of the light ray. This is done at a convenient distance from the plan, as shown. The true inclination of the light ray is drawn passing through the centre of the sphere in this elevation and then the elevation of the line of separation is drawn at right-angles to the actual light ray. (For obvious reasons the line of separation on the elevation will pass through the centre of the circle representing the elevation of the sphere.)

Step 3. The plan view of the line of separation is located by simple projection from the elevation.

Step 4. Because the line of separation on the surface of the sphere will divide the sphere exactly in halves, i.e. one half will be seen in light and the other in shade, an imaginary plane can be placed through the sphere to coincide with the line of separation. The line of separation will appear as a circle on that plane, so if the imaginary plane is located, its shadow can easily be located together with its main axes and diagonals. This plane is located first in the elevation by constructing the square containing the circle representing the sphere in elevation and then continuing the elevation of the line of separation to meet its sides (top and bottom). This inclined plane is then located in the plan view by normal projection. From the plan view this inclined plane can be sighted and projected up and located in the perspective view in the usual way.

Step 5. When the inclined plane is located in the perspective view it should be remembered that this plane in its present form does not represent a square in perspective which contains the circle (line of separation) but the original plane located in the elevation. The actual square is located by projecting the intersections of the elevation of the line of separation and the circumference of the circle to the plan and then up to the perspective. Then the diagonals and axes of the square can be located and drawn. When this is done, the ellipse representing the line of separation on the surface of the sphere in perspective can be drawn, using normal projection up from the plan.

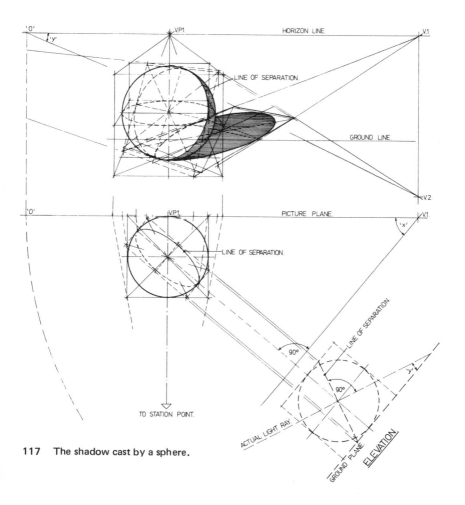

117 The shadow cast by a sphere.

Step 6. Using V.1 and V.2, the shadow of the inclined plane can be located and drawn on the ground plane. On this shadow of the inclined plane, the shadow of the square containing the circle (the line of separation), together with its axes and diagonals, can be located in perspective.

Step 7. Once the shadow of the square and its axes and diagonals are drawn in the perspective view, the points of intersection of the line of separation on the surface of the perspective view of the sphere and the axes and diagonals of the inclined plane can be located in the shadow by using V.1 and V.2 in the normal way.

Step 8. By joining up the shadow points of the intersections of the line of separation and the axes and diagonals of the inclined plane, the shadow of the sphere is drawn as shown.

Though the diagram explaining the construction of the shadow of a sphere looks somewhat complex, if the eight steps described here are followed, the construction will prove to be simpler than it looks. In reality the shadow of a sphere can be described as the shadow of its line of separation, which is simply a circle inclined to both the ground and picture planes. Once this is understood it can be seen that most of the construction shown is needed to locate the inclined plane coinciding with the line of separation, while the construction needed for the actual shadow of the line of separation is very little different from that for any other disk seen in perspective.

Before concluding this section on shadows cast by sunlight, it is worth repeating some of the more important rules for the construction of shadows in perspective projection. The shadow of a vertical line will be cast in the direction of the light ray. If the vertical line is standing on the ground plane its shadow will start from its point of intersection with the ground plane and finish with the first light ray which can pass unobstructed over the top of it. The only time that the shadow of a vertical line does not start from its intersection with the ground plane (or any plane parallel to the ground plane) is when the line does not meet the ground plane. In this case it is necessary to locate the point where it would meet the ground plane if extended (i.e. its plan position) before the shadow of that line can be cast. Perhaps the greatest time-saver in shadow projection is the fact that parallel lines cast parallel shadows. It should be remembered that the line of separation is an extremely important line because the shadow of an object is in reality the shadow of its line of separation. Probably this could be seen most clearly in the shadow of a sphere (Fig.117) but if all of the other examples in this section are examined it will be seen that this is always the case; therefore, if in doubt as to the correctness of the shadow cast by an object, locate its line of separation and check the result obtained.

Finally, shade and shadow in perspective projection are the result of correct construction allied to common sense and the ability of the student to understand three-dimensional representation.

The second type of light source is the artificial, which differs from sunlight in that the light rays from the sun are considered to be parallel whereas those emanating from an artificial source, in their simplest form, radiate from a single point. Fig.118 shows a simple artificial light source with light rays radiating from it. From this diagram it can be seen that because these light rays radiate, i.e. the further away from the light source they are, the further apart they will be, the shadows cast by artificial light must differ from those cast by sunlight. However, this difference is not as great as might be expected. Light rays from an artificial light source, though not parallel, have in all other respects the same qualities as light rays from the sun. They travel in straight lines, they cannot change direction unless a reflector is introduced, they cannot pass through solid opaque matter, in other words, everything to do with individual light rays and their properties remains the same whether they originate from the sun or from an artificial source. Therefore the difference between shadows cast by sunlight and artificial light will be limited to size only. The shape will remain the same but because light rays from an artifical source are not parallel, but in fact get further apart as they travel away from their source, it should be readily understood that a shadow cast by them will be larger than that cast by parallel light rays.

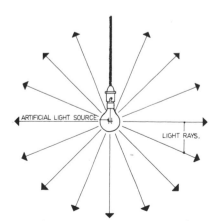

ARTIFICIAL LIGHT SOURCE

LIGHT RAYS.

118   An artificial light source is regarded as a point source, unlike the sun, whose rays are, for all practical purposes, parallel.

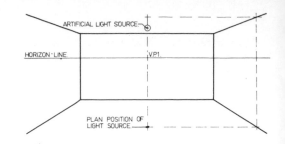

ARTIFICIAL LIGHT SOURCE

HORIZON · LINE   V.P1.

**119   Locating an artificial
light source.**

PLAN POSITION OF
LIGHT SOURCE

The actual construction of shadows cast by artificial light is
very similar to that used for the construction of shadows cast by
sunlight inasmuch as they both rely on the intersection of an actual
light ray and its plan to locate a shadow point. Because light rays
from the sun are parallel it was necessary to locate vanishing points
for the actual light rays and for their plans. Light rays from an artificial light source are not parallel; therefore vanishing points are not
required. The light source can be located as shown in Fig.119 and,
because plans of the light rays from this source are necessary, the
plan position of that light source will have to be located. The artificial light source in Fig.119 is shown located in a room which was
set up using one-point perspective construction in the usual way
(construction not shown). The plan position of the artificial light
source is shown located in the floor plane by simple projection.

The four examples shown in Fig.120 have been set up in the
same way as the one shown in Fig.119 and have the same artificial
light source. Fig.120a shows a single light ray, drawn at random,
together with its plan. From this it should be possible to see the
similarity between this type of construction and that used for constructing shadows in sunlight.

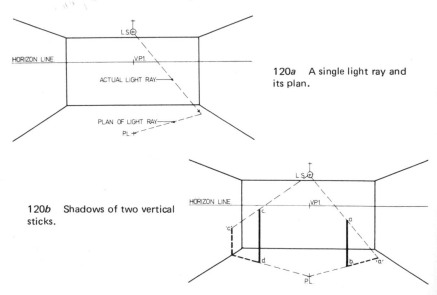

L S

HORIZON LINE   V.P1.

ACTUAL LIGHT RAY

PLAN OF LIGHT RAY

PL

**120a   A single light ray and
its plan.**

**120b   Shadows of two vertical
sticks.**

L S

HORIZON LINE   V.P1.

PL.

Fig.120*b* shows a single stick *ab* standing on the floor. To locate the shadow of this stick it is necessary to draw the plan of the light ray from the plan location (P.L.) of the light source, through the base of the stick *(b)*. From the artificial light source (L.S.) a light ray is drawn through the top of the stick *(a)* and continued to meet the plan line. The intersection of these two lines will be the shadow point of *a*. Therefore the shadow of the stick *ab* will be that part of the plan of the light ray between the base of the stick *(b)* and the shadow point *'a'*. The stick *cd* is placed closer to one of the walls of the room so that its shadow will not only appear on the floor but will also 'run up the wall'. The plan line is drawn from the plan location of the artificial light source (P.L.) through the base of the stick *(d)* until it meets the intersection of the horizontal floor plane and the vertical wall plane, where it will continue up the wall vertically (parallel lines cast parallel shadows) until it meets the actual light ray drawn from the artificial light source (L.S.). In this way point *'c'*, which is the shadow of the top of the stick, is located on the wall.

In Fig.120*c* there are two sticks again but this time they are horizontal, fixed at right-angles to the side walls of the room. As with shadows cast by the sun, it is necessary to locate the plan position of the object casting the shadow when that object is no longer located in the ground plane. Once the plans of these two sticks are located on the floor the shadows can be constructed in the normal way. Stick *ab* is dealt with first because its shadow is slightly simpler than the other one. First, the plan of the light ray is drawn from P.L. through the plan of end *b* of stick *ab*. The actual light ray is then drawn from L.S. through end *b* to meet the plan of the

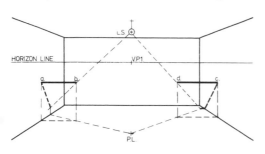

120*c*   Shadows of two horizontal sticks.

120*d*   Vertical and horizontal sticks combined.

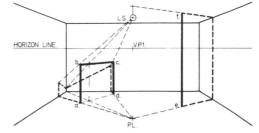

light ray which has 'run up the wall'. This point of intersection between the light ray and its plan will be the shadow of end *b*. The shadow of stick *ab* will start from the point where it joins the wall *(a)* and finish at the shadow of end *b*; therefore the shadow is drawn as a line joining these two points.

Stick *cd* is placed lower down the wall, which means that a part of its shadow will fall on the floor plane. Again the plan of the light ray is drawn from P.L. through the plan position of end *d*. The actual light ray which is then drawn from L.S. through end *d* will meet the plan of the light ray on the floor plane; this means that the shadow of end *d* will fall in the floor plane while end *c* will be located in the wall plane. Again it should be remembered that parallel lines cast parallel shadows, which means that from the shadow point of end *d* the shadow of the stick, while it is cast on the floor, will be parallel to the stick. When the shadow reaches the wall it will no longer be parallel and will in fact run up the wall in a straight line from its intersection with the wall to point *c*.

The fourth example in this figure (Fig.120*d*) shows two different objects located in the room. The first is a vertical stick which touches the ceiling at point *f* and the floor at point *e*. The plan of the light ray is drawn from P.L. through end *e* in the normal way until it meets the wall of the room, where it will continue up the wall. Because the top of the stick (point *f*) is in the ceiling plane, which is above the artificial light source, a part of the shadow of stick *ef* will of course fall on the ceiling. Because the conditions will be much the same as those for the shadow falling on the floor it will be necessary to locate the 'plan' position of the light source on the ceiling. Once this is done, a line representing a plan of the light ray (on the ceiling) can be drawn from this plan position through end *f* and continued to the wall, where it will join up with the plan line from end *e* in the floor plane. This means that the shadow of stick *ef* will extend from point *f* on the ceiling across to the wall, where it will continue down the wall vertically (parallel lines ... etc.) and back across the floor to point *e* in the floor plane.

The other object in Fig.120*d* is in the form of a stool which is placed so that line *bc* is not parallel to the walls of the room. The two vertical lines of the object, *ab* and *dc*, are simple vertical lines and can be dealt with as described in Fig.120*b*. The horizontal line *bc* is a little more difficult in this example because it no longer casts a shadow on a plane parallel to it; in fact it will cast a part of its shadow on each of the two walls. The easiest and quickest way to construct this shadow is to draw a plan of the light ray from the intersection of the two walls back to P.L. At the point where this plan of the light ray intersects the plan of line *bc* a vertical projection is made to locate this point on the line *bc*. An actual light ray drawn from L.S. through this point will locate the intersection of the two parts of the shadow of *bc* on the line of intersection of the two walls. If this point is then joined to the shadows of the tops of the two vertical sticks this will result in the shadow of horizontal stick *bc* on the two walls.

The four examples in Fig.120 dealt with simple sticks. Fig.121 consists of another four examples but in this case planes instead of sticks are used. Fig.121*a* shows a horizontal plane (such as a small table) placed directly beneath the artificial light source. The plan location (P.L.) is located as previously described and is used to draw the plans of the light rays through the plan locations of the four corners of the horizontal plane. The actual light rays are drawn from L.S. through the corners of the horizontal plane to meet their plans. The shadow of the horizontal plane is drawn by joining up the four intersections of the light rays and their plans. Fig.121*b* shows two horizontal planes cantilevered from the walls. In both cases, before the shadows can be cast it is necessary to locate plans of the planes on the floor. Once this is done their shadows can be constructed by using the L.S. and the P.L. in the normal way.

Fig.121*c* shows two vertical planes, one of which extends from the floor to the ceiling and has a rectangular hole in it. By reference to Fig.120*d* the main shadow of the plane can be located. The hole is located simply by locating its plan position by vertical projection. Once this is done, plans of light rays are drawn and projected up the wall to meet the actual light rays drawn from L.S. through the four corners of the hole. The other vertical plane is dealt with initially in much the same way as a simple vertical stick. The shadow of the nearer vertical edge of the plane is located by drawing the plan of the light ray from P.L. to the wall and then up the wall until it meets the actual light ray. The shadow of the top of the plane is simply drawn parallel (in perspective) to the top of the plane until it meets the 'back' wall of the room where it changes direction and joins up to the point of intersection of the top of the plane and the wall.

Fig.121*d* shows an inclined plane resting against a vertical plane. The shadow cast by the vertical plane is constructed in the normal way, using plans of light rays from P.L. and actual light rays from L.S. The plan of the inclined plane will be required before its shadow can be located. If the shadow of the inclined plane and the

123

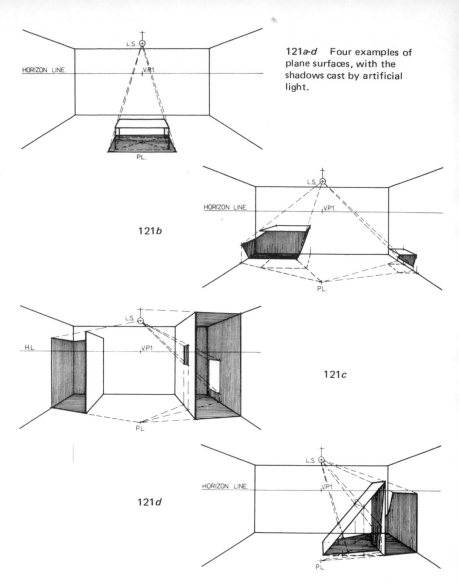

121a-d   Four examples of plane surfaces, with the shadows cast by artificial light.

121b

121c

121d

shadow of the vertical plane fell on the floor plane it would be a simple matter of joining the points of the shadow of the top of the vertical plane to the points where the inclined plane met the floor. However, in this example the shadows are cast not only on the floor but also on two walls. This means that it is necessary to locate some arbitrary points on the inclined plane so that the shadows of these points can be located. By joining up these points the correct shadow of the structure can be drawn.

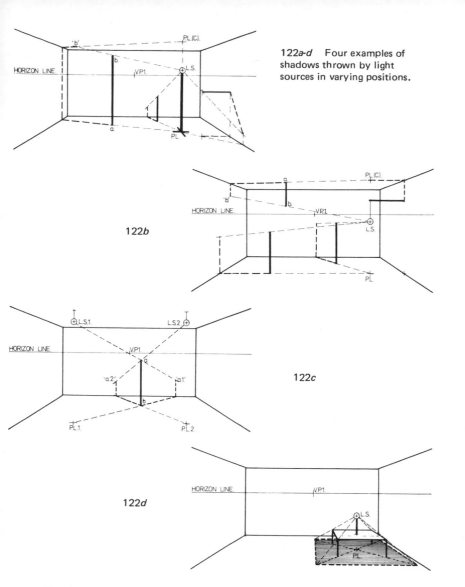

122a-d Four examples of shadows thrown by light sources in varying positions.

122b

122c

122d

The four examples shown in Fig.120 and the four in Fig.121 all used an artificial light source located in the same position in the room and slightly below the ceiling. Fig.122 consists of a further four examples in which different positions are used for the light source. Fig.122a shows a light source consistent with a standard lamp on a floor pedestal. This type of light source simplifies the location of the plan location of the light source (P.L.). The short stick is treated in exactly the same way as the previous ones. The

125

horizontal stick is also self-explanatory. The taller stick *(ab)* requires a plan location of the artificial light source on the ceiling so that the shadow of end *b* can be located on the ceiling as shown. Fig. 122*b* shows a light source suspended from a horizontal stick located on one of the walls. This means that the stick supporting the L.S. will cast a shadow on the ceiling so again the plan position of the L.S. will be required on the ceiling. Once this is done the shadow will be obvious, as should be the shadows of the vertical sticks located on the floor. The short stick located on the ceiling is a little different from the others. Its shadow is located using the plan location of the light source on the ceiling and the actual light ray.

Fig. 122*c* shows a slight variation in which two artificial light sources are used. This means that each will cast a shadow of the stick; therefore each will require its plan location on the floor plane. The two shadows are cast in the normal way. Fig. 122*d* shows a table lamp located on a low table. The plan location of the artificial light source is located on the floor in the normal way. Using this P.L. to draw the plans of the light rays through the four corners of the plan of the table, to intersect the actual light rays from the L.S. through the four corners of the table, its shadow can be drawn as shown.

The twelve examples in the preceding three figures cover most of the possibilities likely to be encountered either directly or indirectly when the subject consists of straight lines, that is to say a problem may consist of either combinations of the examples shown or simple adaptations of them.

Fig. 123 shows a disk suspended above the ground plane, set up with a one-point perspective construction as previously described. (The construction lines have been omitted, to avoid unnecessary confusion.) An artificial light source has been located directly above the centre of the circle. As with all other shadow projections, when an object is suspended above the ground plane it is necessary to locate a plan of the object on the ground plane in the perspective view. Here this is done in the normal way, using a perspective view of the square containing the circle together with its diagonals. Because the light source is located directly above the centre of the circle, the plan location of the light source will be at the intersection of the diagonals of the square surrounding the plan of the circle. As in the construction of a shadow of a disk in sunlight (Fig. 114), it is necessary to locate the shadow of the square containing the circle before the shadow of the disk can be drawn. To obtain the

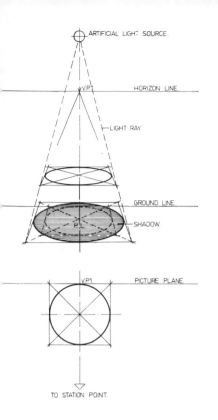

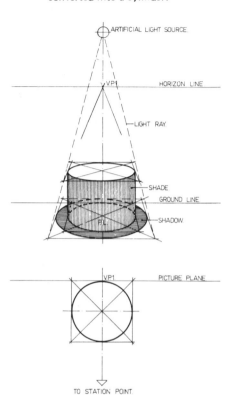

124 The suspended disk of Fig. 123, converted into a cylinder.

123 The shadow of a suspended disk, cast by artificial light.

shadow of the square containing the shadow of the disk it is necessary to draw the plans of the light rays from P.L. through the four corners of the plan of the square containing the plan of the disk. (In this case these plans of the light rays will coincide with the diagonals.) Actual light rays are then drawn from the light source through the four corners of the square containing the disk to meet the appropriate plan lines, and these points of intersection are then joined up as shown. The shadow of the disk is then drawn by projecting actual light rays from the light source through the intersections of the ellipse representing the disk in perspective and the diagonals of the square surrounding it, to meet the diagonals of the square surrounding the shadow. The ellipse representing the shadow of the disk is then drawn by joining up these points on the diagonals. The shadow of the disk will in fact be circular because

127

the disk is parallel to the ground plane, and therefore it will be seen as a true ellipse in the perspective view. Because the light rays emanate from a single point the shadow of the disk, for obvious reasons, will appear larger than the disk itself.

Fig.124 shows a cylinder set up using one-point perspective construction as previously described. An artificial light source is located directly above the centre of the circular end of the cylinder. Because the construction of the shadow in this example is identical to the one described in Fig.123, there is no need to repeat it. Sufficient to say that the sides of the cylinder will be seen in shade. This must be so because the light source is situated directly above the centre of the circular end of the cylinder, which means that the line of separation will be around the edge of the circular end.

Fig.125 shows a sphere set up using one-point perspective construction as previously described. The light source is located directly above the centre of the sphere. It is necessary to locate the line of separation on the surface of the sphere in perspective before the

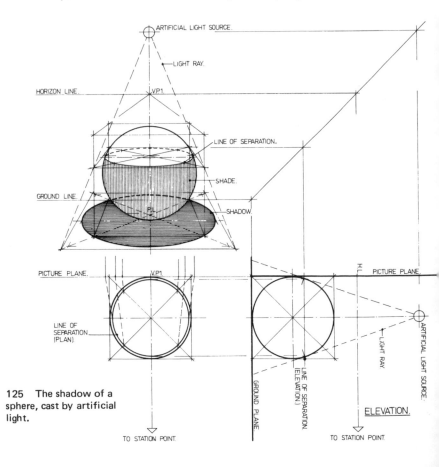

125 The shadow of a sphere, cast by artificial light.

shadow of the sphere can be located and drawn. Before this can be done it is necessary to locate the line of separation on the plan view of the sphere, which means that an elevation will be required, set up at a convenient distance from the plan. By drawing the actual light rays from the light source in the elevation, an elevation of the line of separation can be located. This line of separation is then located on the plan view of the sphere by simple projection. By locating a plane through the sphere to coincide with the line of separation in the elevation it is possible to locate this plane in the perspective view. By projecting up from the plan in the normal way, the ellipse representing the line of separation can be drawn on this plane which was located to coincide with the line of separation. This means that the ellipse is in reality on the surface of the sphere. Once the line of separation is located it is a simple matter to draw the shadow of that line of separation in exactly the same way as that described for the two preceding examples. The shadow will again be much larger than the line of separation, for the same obvious reasons.

Before concluding this section, it is worth looking at the shadow cast by a cylinder when the light source is located in a position other than directly over the centre of the circular end. Fig.126 shows the same cylinder as was used in Fig. 124 set up as before but with an artificial light source located above and to one side of it. As with the previous examples, it is necessary to find the plan location of the

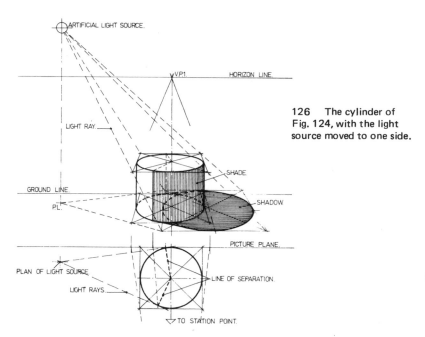

126   The cylinder of Fig. 124, with the light source moved to one side.

light source before the shadow of the cylinder can be constructed. Once this is done the construction is much the same as the previous ones, i.e. the plans of the light rays are drawn from P.L. through the four corners of the perspective view of the square surrounding the base of the cylinder (the base corresponds to the plan). When the actual light rays are drawn through the corners of the square surrounding the top circular end of the cylinder, the square surrounding the shadow of the top of the cylinder can be drawn in perspective. The actual shadow of the top of the cylinder is drawn in the normal way by using actual light rays through the intersections of the ellipse forming the end of the cylinder and the diagonals of the square surrounding it.

The line of separation is a little more complicated in this case. The line of separation of a cylinder is always at right-angles to the light rays, as previously explained. While the light rays were parallel, as for sunlight, this was a simple matter because the line of separation would have to be a diameter of the circle. In the example shown here, the light rays are no longer parallel and, because the line of separation is at right-angles to the light rays, it will no longer be a diameter of the circle. Because the light rays form tangents to the circumference of the circle, the line of separation which is at right-angles to the light rays will pass through the centre of the circle; this means that the line of separation will be as shown in Fig. 126. If this is compared with the line of separation of the cylinder in Fig.115 this basic difference between the two sets of conditions should be much clearer. The other main difference is that the shadow cast by the artificial light source will become wider as it travels away from the object whereas the sides of the shadow cast by sunlight will remain parallel. There are, of course, other differences but these should be obvious to the serious student so it is not necessary to elaborate them.

In summing up, it can be fairly said that shadows are a combination of simple construction, common sense and a reasonable understanding of the two-dimensional representation of three-dimensional objects. If the basic principles are understood, shadows can be constructed on drawings of the most complex subjects without any difficulty. A reliable, accurate short-cut method for locating the vanishing points for the plans of the light rays and the actual light rays is shown in the next chapter but like most other short cuts it is of little use unless it is fully understood; therefore the student is advised to learn the basic principles before adopting this or any other short cut.

9 Short cuts in perspective drawing

Before proceeding with the final chapter of this book it is important to point out that any short cut in perspective projection which is not based on sound principles is no short cut at all but an expression of ignorance of the subject. The short cut is essential today because many of the basic methods, when applied to large, complex objects, become somewhat unwieldy and time-consuming, and thus unacceptable commercially. This is no reason to cast aside accuracy in the two-dimensional representation of three-dimensional objects, but rather a challenge to the student to acquire the knowledge and skill to produce a commodity which is acceptable in the commercial world, which he is destined to enter at the conclusion of his studies.

I propose, therefore, to introduce a number of basic short cuts and relate them back to sound principles, so that the student can use them with confidence and without loss of accuracy. The ones shown are not by any means a complete catalogue of short cuts: many of them can be adapted and/or extended to cover many problems which may be encountered, but if they are thoroughly understood this will be a comparatively simple matter.

The first of these short cuts is a two-point construction which, under certain conditions, can save a great deal of time and space. This particular short cut is divided into two parts, the first of which is the setting up of a simple cube using two-point perspective when the cube is located with its front edge (the one nearest the spectator) coinciding with the picture plane and its sides at 45° to that picture plane. Fig.127 shows the normal method used to construct a perspective view of a cube under the conditions described here using a plan construction. If the resulting perspective view is examined certain facts are discernible, the first of which is that the two sides of the cube facing the spectator are of equal width (the sides are at 45° to the picture plane), which means that the vanishing points are at equal distances from the centre line of vision (which coincides with the front edge of the cube). The second of these facts is that because the front edge of the cube coincides with the picture

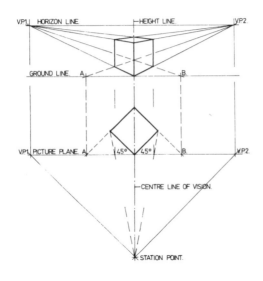

127 Two-point perspective
view of a cube seen edge-on.

128 Two-point perspective
view of a cube seen edge-on.

plane it can be used as the height line. The height of the object can
be measured on this line using its true scale height which means that
the front edge of the cube in the perspective view will be the true
scale height of the cube. The third of these discernible facts is that
because the two sides seen by the spectator are of equal width the
back edge of the cube will fall directly behind the front edge.

Fig.128 shows one other useful piece of information with regard
to a cube located with its front edge coinciding with the picture
plane and its sides at $45°$ to the picture plane. The two sides forming

132

the back of the cube as seen by the spectator can be extended forward to meet the picture plane as shown. If the points of intersection of these extended sides of the cube and the picture plane are projected up vertically to the ground line (points *A* and *B*) and these points in the ground line are joined to the appropriate vanishing points, i.e. *A* to V.P.2 and *B* to V.P.1, the bottom edges of the sides forming the back of the cube in perspective, as seen by the spectator, will fall in these lines.

If the three facts from Fig.127 and the one from Fig.128 are put together it is possible to use them to set up a perspective view of a cube when its front edge is located in the picture plane and its sides are at 45° to the picture plane. Fig.129 shows how this is done when the horizon line in the perspective view is also used as a picture plane.

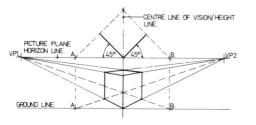

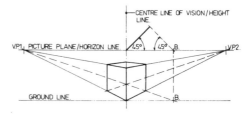

129   Perspective view of a cube seen edge-on; simplified method.

130   Perspective view of a cube: the method of Fig. 129, simplified one stage further.

If this diagram is compared with those in Fig. 127 and Fig.128 it can be seen that all of the conditions are fulfilled; therefore the result obtained is identical. This construction shown in Fig.129 can be simplified further, as shown in Fig.130 where the result obtained is again identical to those obtained in Figs. 127, 128 and 129. The short-cut method of setting up a perspective view of a cube with its front edge located in the picture plane and its sides at 45° to the picture plane is shown in Fig. 131 and is as follows:

Step 1. In a convenient position on the sheet of paper draw a horizontal line to represent the horizon line in the perspective view. Near each end of the horizon line locate a vanishing point (V.P.1

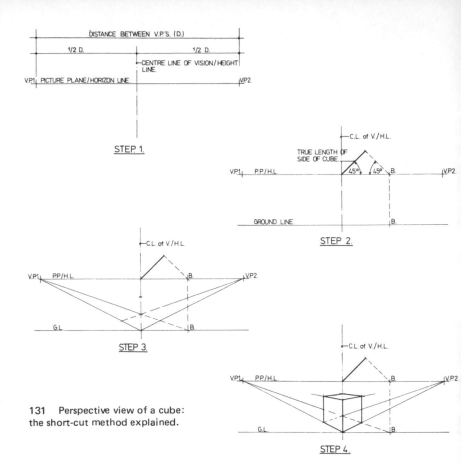

131 Perspective view of a cube:
the short-cut method explained.

and V.P.2). Divide the distance between the two vanishing points
exactly in half and draw a vertical line representing the centre line
of vision (which coincides with the front edge of the cube, which
is also the height line).

Step 2. Locate the ground line at the required distance below the
horizon line. (The ground line is located with regard to the view
of the cube required and the limits of the cone of vision — both
subjects to be dealt with separately later.) From the intersection
of the centre line of vision/height line and the picture plane/
horizon line, a side of the cube is set out at 45° to the picture
plane/horizon line. The extension of the side forming the back of
the cube is also set out at 45° to the P.P./H.L. The intersection of
the extended side and the P.P./H.L. (point *B*) is located in the
ground line by vertical projection in the normal way. (The side

of the cube can be set out on either side of the centre line of vision/height line.)

Step 3. From the intersection of the centre line of vision/height line and the ground line, lines are drawn back to V.P.1 and V.P.2. From point *B* in the ground line a line is drawn back to V.P.1 and from the intersection of this line and the centre line of vision/height line a line is drawn back to V.P.2, which completes the base of the cube in the perspective view. The height of the cube, measured from the ground line up, is then located on the centre line of vision/height line.

Step 4. Complete the sides and the top of the cube using the appropriate vanishing points.

Because the distance between the two vanishing points and the distance between the horizon line and the ground line are the same in this example as in the four preceding ones the result obtained will be identical. However, it should be understood that the distance between the vanishing points is arbitrary within the limits of the cone of vision i.e. if the vanishing points are too close together this will present a very close station point which could result in a distorted view of the cube. The further apart the vanishing points are placed the further the spectator is from the object viewed. Similarly, the further apart the horizon line and the ground line are placed the higher the eye-level of the spectator; therefore the distance between the horizon line and the ground line is also an arbitrary dimension, within the limits of the cone of vision.

Before exploring the value of being able to set up, quickly and accurately, a cube under these conditions in perspective projection it is necessary to examine the second part of this short cut. If a cube is again located with its front edge (the one nearest to the spectator) coinciding with the picture plane and the centre line of vision, but in this case with its sides making angles of 60° and 30° with the picture plane, it is again possible to set up a perspective view of the cube using a short-cut method similar to that shown in Fig.131. The normal method used for constructing a perspective view of a cube under these conditions is shown in Fig.132. By examining the resulting perspective view of the cube obtained in Fig.132 a number of facts can be discerned. The first of these is that the side adjacent to the 30° angle will appear to the spectator to be twice as wide as the side adjacent to the 60° angle. The second of these facts is that

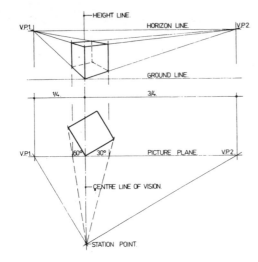

132   Cube with sides at 60°
and 30° to the picture plane:
normal method of two-point
perspective construction.

the centre line of vision/height line (which coincides with the front
edge of the cube) is located at one-quarter of the distance between
the vanishing points (V.P.1 and V.P.2), this one-quarter being on the
side adjacent to the 60° angle. Obviously the other three-quarters of
the distance between the vanishing points will be on the side adjacent to the 30° angle. The third of these discernible facts is that
because the front edge of the cube is located in the picture plane it
can be used as the height line and because it coincides with the centre line of vision, locating the centre line of vision also locates the
height line.

133   The cube of Fig. 132,
with two sides extended to the
picture plane (compare Fig.
128).

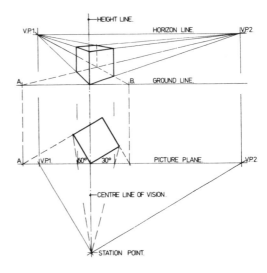

Fig.133 shows in plan the two sides forming the back of the cube, as seen by the spectator, extended forward to meet the picture plane at points A and B. If the points of intersection of these extended sides are projected up vertically to the ground line and lines are drawn from them back to the appropriate vanishing points (from point A back to V.P.2 and from point B back to V.P.1), the bottom edges of the sides forming the back of the cube, as seen by the spectator, will fall in these lines.

If the facts obtained from Figs. 132 and 133 are put together it is possible to use them to set up a perspective view of a cube when its front edge is located in the picture plane and coincides with the centre line of vision, one of its sides makes an angle of 60° with the picture plane and another side makes an angle of 30° with the picture plane. Fig.134 shows how this is done without using the set-up shown in Fig.132. This short-cut method of setting up a perspective view of the cube is shown in Fig.135 and as follows:

Step 1. In a convenient position on the sheet of paper draw a horizontal line to represent the horizon line in the perspective view. Near each end of the horizon line locate a vanishing point (V.P.1 and V.P.2) as shown. Divide the distance between V.P.1 and V.P.2 into four equal parts and draw a vertical line through one of the quarter divisions so that the distance between the vanishing points is divided in the proportion of one-quarter to three-quarters. This line represents the centre line of vision (which coincides with the front edge of the cube and the height line).

Step 2. Locate the ground line at the required distance below the horizon line. (The ground line is located with regard to the view of the cube required and the limits of the cone of vision — both subjects dealt with separately later.) From the intersection of the centre line of vision/height line and the picture plane/horizon line, a side of the cube is drawn at 60° to the picture plane/horizon line on the side with the shortest distance between the centre

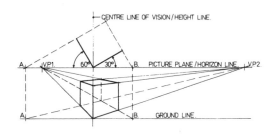

134   The cube of Fig. 132: perspective view of the short-cut method.

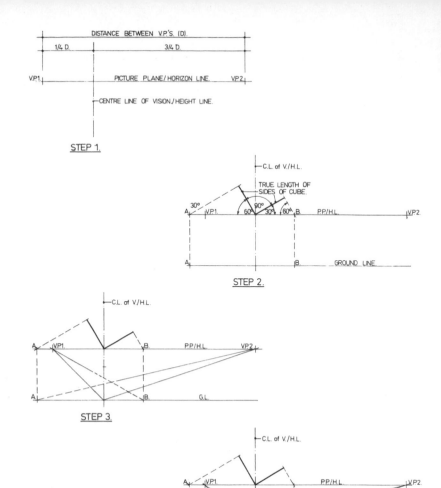

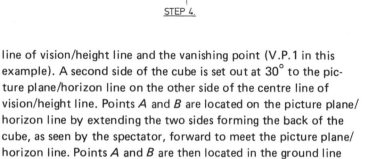

135 The short-cut method step
by step.

line of vision/height line and the vanishing point (V.P.1 in this
example). A second side of the cube is set out at 30° to the picture plane/horizon line on the other side of the centre line of
vision/height line. Points *A* and *B* are located on the picture plane/
horizon line by extending the two sides forming the back of the
cube, as seen by the spectator, forward to meet the picture plane/
horizon line. Points *A* and *B* are then located in the ground line
by vertical projection in the normal way.

Step 3. From the intersection of the centre line of vision/height line and the ground line, lines are drawn back to V.P.1 and V.P.2. From points *A* and *B* lines are drawn back to V.P.1 and V.P.2 to complete the base of the cube in the perspective view. The height of the cube is then located on the centre line of vision/ height line (measured from the ground line up.)

Step 4. Complete the sides and the top of the cube, using the appropriate vanishing points.

Because all of the circumstances in this example are the same as those in Figs. 132, 133 and 134 the result obtained is identical. The similarity between this short cut and the one shown in Fig.131 will be readily seen; therefore it is unnecessary to repeat the observations which follow the description of that figure. Sufficient to say that either of the two ends can be used for the one-quarter division, depending on the view of the cube required.

Because the results obtained by both of these short-cut methods are identical to the result obtained using the normal construction, they can be considered accurate and therefore acceptable. However, it should be remembered that they are accurate only for the two sets of conditions described, and are useless in their present form for any other conditions. As with any other perspective construction, one of the most important steps is the use of the cone of vision to check the limits of the drawing so that distortions can be avoided. Neither of the two short-cut methods shown here has a plan construction as such, with a station point etc., which means that it is necessary to devise an alternative method for checking against distortions such as an object or a part of an object falling outside the cone of vision. To understand this alternative method or short cut it is necessary first to examine the construction shown in Fig.136 where the same cube is set up in perspective construction under the same conditions as the one in Fig.127. The cone of vision is shown in the plan in the normal way and the area which the cone of vision covers on the picture plane is also shown. By examination it will be found that the radius of the area covered by the cone of vision is slightly more than one-quarter of the distance between the two vanishing points; therefore if one-quarter of that distance is used it will provide a safe margin for the student. Similarly in Fig.137, where a $60^{\circ}/30^{\circ}$ set-up is used, the cone of vision covers an area whose radius is one-quarter of the distance between the two vanishing points.

If it is known that on the picture plane the cone of vision covers

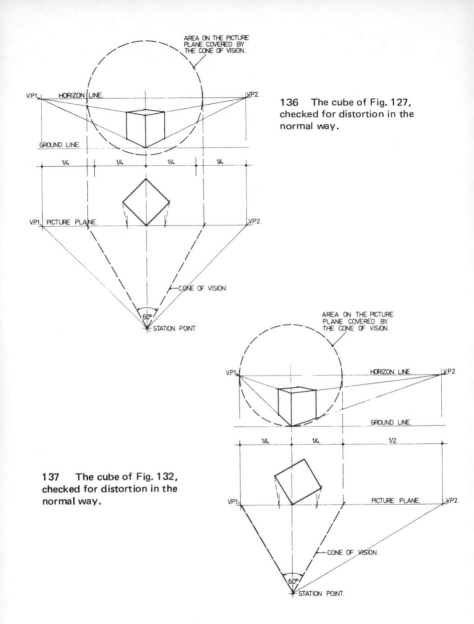

136 The cube of Fig. 127, checked for distortion in the normal way.

137 The cube of Fig. 132, checked for distortion in the normal way.

a circle whose radius is equal to one-quarter of the distance between the vanishing points, this can be located in the short-cut method, as shown in Figs. 138 and 139 where the horizontal limits of the drawing can be located simply by measurement. The vertical limits are also located by simple measurement as shown in Figs. 140 and 141. In both cases the intersection between the centre line of vision/

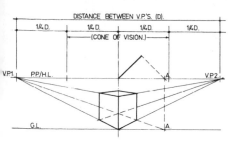

138   The cube of Fig. 131, checked for distortion by the short-cut method: the circular field of the cone of vision is reduced to a straight line (the diameter).

139   The cube of Fig. 135, checked for distortion by the short-cut method.

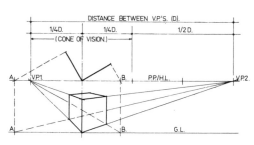

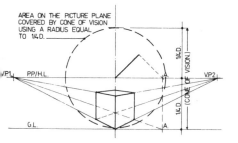

140   Locating the vertical limits by measurement.

141   Locating the vertical limits by measurement.

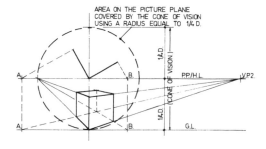

height line and the horizon line is used as the starting point for measuring both the horizontal and the vertical limits of the cone of vision.

From the examples shown in Figs.127 through to 141, using these short-cut methods, which are quicker to carry out than to describe, it can be seen that it is possible to produce quickly a reli-

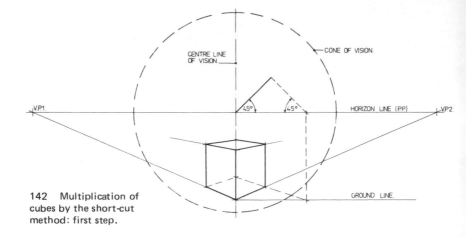

142 Multiplication of cubes by the short-cut method: first step.

able, accurate view of a cube in perspective projection. It is reliable because whichever of the two sets of conditions is used the results obtained will always be identical to those obtained with the normal construction methods and those exact conditions. If this is doubted, a few simple experiments will prove convincing for even the most sceptical.

The value of being able to produce an accurate perspective view of a cube under the conditions previously described may not be fully realized until this short-cut method is related to the one explained in Chapter 6, 'Reflections' (see Figs. 64–67), where it was found that by the use of diagonals more identical cubes could be added horizontally, in any direction, to a single cube. To explain this more fully, a single cube is set up in perspective in Fig. 142 using the 45°/45° short-cut method. Fig.143 shows a number of identical faces

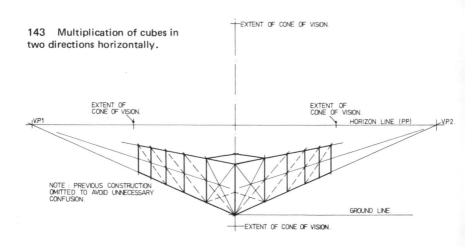

143 Multiplication of cubes in two directions horizontally.

of cubes added to each of the two faces of the original cube seen by the spectator. This is done by locating the centres of the two faces of the original cube (at the intersection of its diagonals). From the centres of the two faces, perspective lines are drawn back to the appropriate vanishing points. Next, each face of the original cube is thought of as half of a rectangle, a diagonal of which will pass through the centre of that rectangle. Therefore, a diagonal drawn from the appropriate corner of the face of the original cube through the intersection of the perspective line from the centre of that face and the side opposite to the corner will intersect an extension of the top edge of the face of the original cube. This point of intersection locates the other end of the rectangle of which the face of the original cube constitutes one half. This means that the other half, which was located by using the diagonal of the rectangle, will be identical to the original half (seen in perspective). In other words, the face of a second cube, identical to the face of the original cube, has been added. By using this principle a number of faces can be added to either of the two faces of the original cube, as required. The only limiting factors to adding an infinite number of faces are the vertical and horizontal limits of the cone of vision. The additional cubes can be completed by simple perspective projection, which should be obvious, therefore it is not shown in the diagrams.

Fig.144 shows the method used for adding identical cubes vertically. Because the original cube was located with its front edge coinciding with the picture plane, this front edge could be used as the height line. Therefore, to add more cubes vertically is simply a matter of setting out the height of the cube the required number

144 Multiplication of cubes vertically.

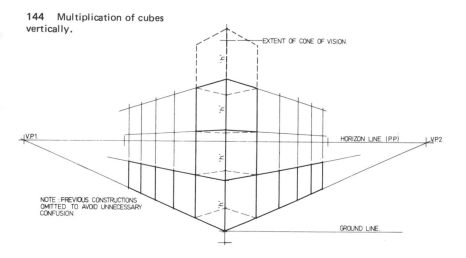

of times and completing the drawings of the additional cubes as shown. In Fig.144 the top cube, which is shown by means of a broken line, falls partly outside the cone of vision which means that normally it will be subject to distortion. However, it will be remembered that in a 45°/45° short-cut method the cone of vision used is slightly smaller than the actual cone of vision; therefore, in this case, the top cube could be drawn and, because it is so close to the limit of the cone of vision, no distortion would be expected.

Once it is possible to set up a number of identical cubes as shown in Fig.144 it is an easy matter to set up a perspective view of any object which can be fitted into a simple cube or a series of cubes. Half-cubes and quarter-cubes can be constructed and used if necessary, which gives the student great flexibility. Little more need be said about the advantages of this short-cut method when it is related back to the 'box' method of drawing objects (Chapter 6).

The foregoing short-cut method of drawing a cube in perspective when it is located with its front edge coinciding with the picture plane and its sides at either 45°/45° or 60°/30° to the picture plane can be extended to rectangular prisms, which can be set up in perspective using the same basic principles. Fig. 145 shows a rectangular

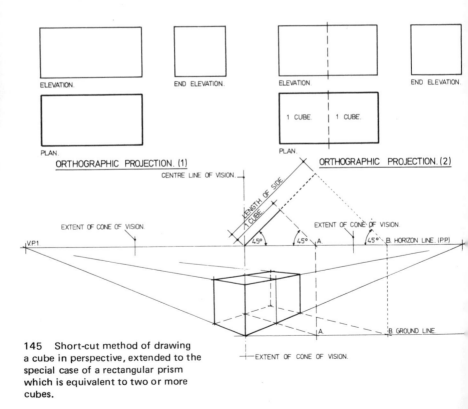

145 Short-cut method of drawing a cube in perspective, extended to the special case of a rectangular prism which is equivalent to two or more cubes.

prism in orthographic projection (1). When this is analysed it can be seen that, in this case, the rectangular prism is made up of two identical cubes, which are also shown in orthographic projection (2). The method used for setting up the rectangular prism is as follows:

Step 1. In a convenient position on the sheet of paper draw a horizontal line to represent the horizon line/picture plane and locate a vanishing point near each end (V.P.1 and V.P.2). Divide the distance between the vanishing points in half because it is intended to view the object with its sides at 45°/45° to the picture plane in this example. Draw the vertical centre line of vision/height line through this centre measurement and locate the ground line at the required distance below the horizon line/ picture plane. Locate the limits of the cone of vision in the usual way.

Step 2. From the intersection of the horizon line/picture plane and the centre line of vision/height line draw one side of a cube at 45° to the horizon line/picture plane and extend it until it equals the total length of the side of the rectangular prism. From the points indicating the measurement of a side of the cube and a side of the rectangular prism draw lines at right-angles to this line to meet the horizon line/picture plane at *A* and *B* respectively. From these two points project down vertically to locate them on the ground line.

Step 3. Using points *A* and *B* in the ground line and V.P.1 and V.P.2 draw the perspective view of the rectangular prism as previously described.

Fig.146 shows the same rectangular prism as used in Fig.145 set up in perspective when its sides are at 60°/30° to the horizon line/ picture plane. The method in this example will be the same as in the preceding one except for the obvious difference in the angles set up. Also, because it is necessary to set up two sides of the cube when using the 60°/30° method, the second side of the cube is located. From this it can be seen that this method is not limited to cubes or objects made up of a number of cubes but can be used for any object, even those which contain sloping planes.

In the example shown in the orthographic projection (1) in Fig. 147, the object can no longer simply be divided into two cubes but if it is analysed, as shown in the orthographic projection (2), the whole of it, including the sloping planes, can be fitted into a simple rectangular prism. Fig.147 shows the rectangular prism set up in the

145

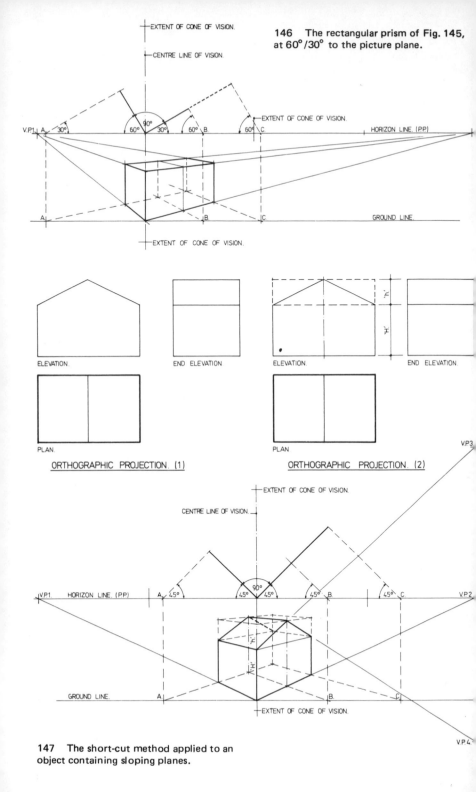

146 The rectangular prism of Fig. 145, at 60°/30° to the picture plane.

ORTHOGRAPHIC PROJECTION. (1)

ORTHOGRAPHIC PROJECTION. (2)

147 The short-cut method applied to an object containing sloping planes.

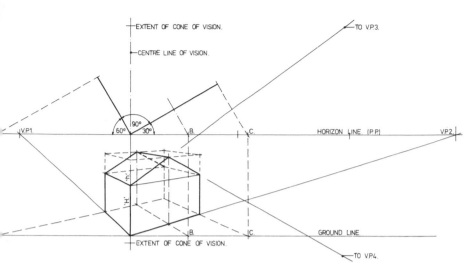

148　The same object, at 60°/30° to the picture plane.

perspective view using the 45°/45° method. Because the object can no longer simply be divided into cubes it is necessary to locate two sides of the rectangular prism. Using the set-up of the rectangular prism which contains the whole of the object, the height of the lower ends of the sloping planes can be measured on the elevation (H) and located on the height line in the perspective construction. This height can then be located on each end of the rectangular prism by projection (in perspective). The centre of the rectangular prism is located from the 'plan' in the normal way and, by joining up the appropriate points in the perspective view, the inclined lines of the inclined planes can be drawn. If these inclined lines are continued to meet a vertical line through the appropriate vanishing point (V.P.2 in this case) vanishing points for these inclined lines can be located (V.P.3 and V.P.4).

Fig. 148 shows the same object as used in Fig. 147 set up using the 60°/30° method. The method should be obvious so it is not necessary to repeat the description; however, the importance of locating vanishing points for inclined lines cannot be over-emphasized. They save a great deal of wasted time and effort and, in many cases, frustration if they are located and used.

Fig. 149 shows another rectangular object with, in this case, a recess in one of its faces as shown in orthographic projection (1). In this case the analysis is fairly simple: the object will not easily

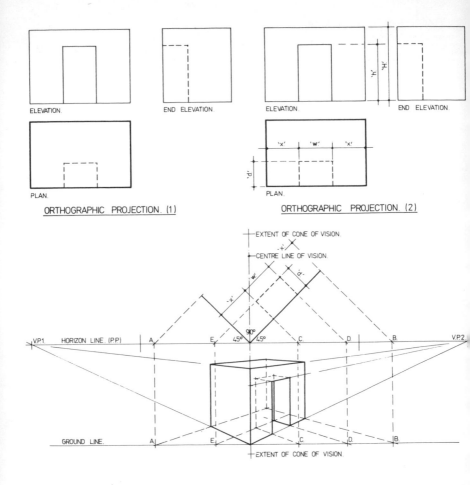

ELEVATION.

END ELEVATION.

ELEVATION.

END ELEVATION.

PLAN.

PLAN.

ORTHOGRAPHIC PROJECTION. (1)

ORTHOGRAPHIC PROJECTION. (2)

EXTENT OF CONE OF VISION.

CENTRE LINE OF VISION.

V.P.1   HORIZON LINE. (P.P)   A   E   45°   45°   C   D   B   V.P.2

90°

GROUND LINE.   A   E   C   D   B

EXTENT OF CONE OF VISION.

149   A rectangular prism with a recess, set up by
the short-cut method.

divide up into cubes, therefore it is necessary to set up a rectangular
prism (two sides) and to locate the height, width and depth of the
recess. The set-up of the rectangular prism using the 45°/45° method
is as previously described. The recess is then set up on the 'plan' as
shown and the same principle is applied to the recess as was applied
to the rectangular prism.   Fig.150 shows the same object set up using
the 60°/30° method, and is self-explanatory.

Once the student can set up accurately a rectangular prism,
inclined planes and simple recesses in perspective projection using

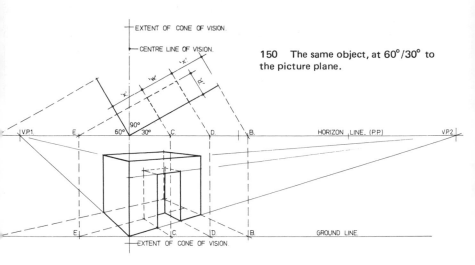

150   The same object, at 60°/30° to the picture plane.

V.P.1.   E.   60° 90° 30°   C.   D.   B.   HORIZON LINE. (P.P.)   V.P.2

GROUND LINE.

EXTENT OF CONE OF VISION.

these methods he should be able to adapt them to any object he is likely to encounter. Though the descriptions and figures have been limited to objects with their front edges coinciding with the picture plane, objects located either behind or in front of the picture plane can be set up in perspective projection using a slight variation of these methods. Fig.151 shows a cube located behind the picture plane. This means that the front edge of the cube is no longer located in the picture plane, therefore it can no longer be used as the height line. The method used for drawing an object in perspective projection when its sides are at 45°/45° to the picture plane and located behind that picture plane is as follows:

Step 1. In a convenient position on the sheet of paper draw a horizontal line to represent the horizon line/picture plane. Locate a vanishing point near each end of the horizon line/picture plane (V.P.1 and V.P.2). Divide the distance between the two vanishing points in half. (It is intended to view the object with its sides at 45°/45° to the picture plane in this example.) Draw the vertical centre line of vision through this centre measurement and locate the ground line at the required distance below the horizon line/picture plane. Locate the limits of the cone of vision in the usual way.

Step 2. Set up two sides of the cube in the required position at 45° to the horizon line/picture plane and project each side to meet the horizon line/picture plane at *A* and *B*. Using vertical pro-

149

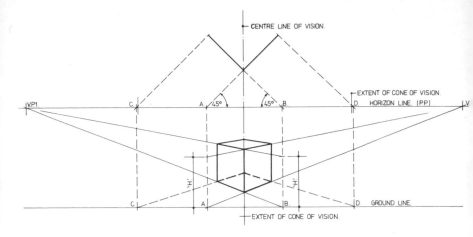

151 The short-cut method applied to a cube located behind the picture plane.

jection, these two points are then located on the ground line. From the other ends of the two sides of the cube, lines are drawn at right-angles to meet the horizon line/picture plane at points *C* and *D*. Because points *A* and *B* are extensions of the two sides of the cube, lines *AA* and *BB* can be used as height lines. The height 'H' of the cube can be set out on each of them, as shown.

Step 3. Using points *A, B, C* and *D* in the ground line and the appropriate vanishing points, draw the perspective view of the cube as previously described.

The 60°/30° method is exactly the same except for the angles of the sides and the division of the horizon line/picture plane, therefore it is not considered necessary to show it. However, the 60°/30° method is used in Fig.152 to explain the construction of a perspective view of a cube located in front of the picture plane. Again the front edge of the cube does not coincide with the picture plane, therefore it cannot be used as the height line. This means that the sides of the 'plan' of the cube will have to be projected back to meet the picture plane before height lines can be obtained. Once the height lines are located the cube can be drawn in the perspective view as shown. This example tends to look 'messy' because the perspective drawing is carried out over the 'plan'. Because of this it is less popular than the other methods, but it is not less accurate or fast than the other methods explained here.

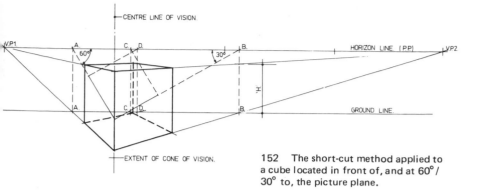

152　The short-cut method applied to a cube located in front of, and at 60°/30° to, the picture plane.

The short-cut methods shown so far have three distinct advantages over what is known as the basic or normal method of perspective projection: (1) They are faster and as accurate; (2) they require less space; and (3) they do not require a complex and time-consuming plan set-up. However, they also have some disadvantages, one of which is that they are limited to two angles for the plan position, 45°/45° or 60°/30°. If this disadvantage is examined reasonably, it will be seen that it is not as limiting as one might think. Each method, i.e. the 45°/45° and the 60°/30° method, allows a choice of four separate views, and it would be agreed that few objects could not be provided for adequately. If a satisfactory view of an object cannot be obtained using these short-cut methods there is always the basic method to fall back on, at least for over-all shapes or units.

The other main disadvantage of these short-cut methods is the difficulty of controlling from the very beginning the ultimate size of the finished drawing. Again, this is not, or need not be, a major disadvantage when the preliminary setting-up of the basic lines of the perspective view is so quick and simple. With a little common sense and practice, the required size of a perspective drawing can be quickly arrived at by trial and error.

Some of the short-cut methods can be combined satisfactorily with the basic or normal method of perspective projection, to speed up the production of a perspective drawing. The 'diagonal' is probably the most useful of all of the short-cut methods because it not only applies to the examples shown so far but has a number of other uses as well. Fig.153 shows how the diagonals can be used to add more identical cubes to one located behind the picture plane. From this example and the others shown in other parts of this book (see Figs. 64–72) it should be obvious that whenever a perspective

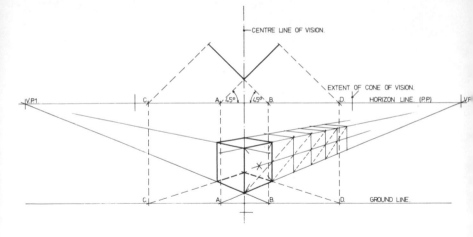

153 Multiplication of a cube located behind the picture plane.

view of an object consists of square or rectangular sides, diagonals can be used either to divide up or to extend those sides.

One important use of the diagonal is the setting-up of a one-point perspective construction using a short-cut method. A basic method of setting up a one-point perspective view of the interior of a room was described in Fig. 77 (p.74), which uses a measuring point (the vanishing point for the diagonals of the square floor tiles). Using the principles involved in the basic method, it is possible to produce exactly the same result using a short-cut method, shown in Fig. 154, as follows:

Step 1. In a convenient position on the sheet of paper draw a horizontal line to represent the horizon line in the perspective view. At a convenient point on this line locate the vanishing point (V.P.) and draw a vertical line through it to represent the centre line of vision.

Step 2. Locate the floor line (ground line) at the required distance below the horizon line. When the floor line has been located it is then possible to draw a true elevation of the end wall of the room. (The end wall of the room in Fig.77 is located in the picture plane.)

Step 3. From the V.P. a line is drawn through each of the four corners of the end wall. These lines represent the intersections

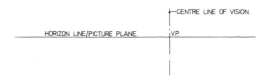

STEP 1.

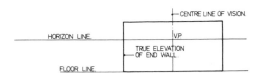

STEP 2.

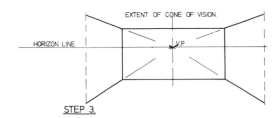

STEP 3.

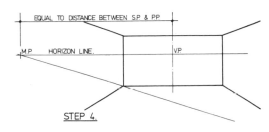

STEP 4.

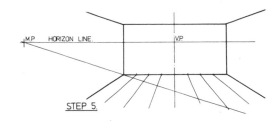

STEP 5.

154 One-point perspective of a room with tiled floor: this is Fig. 77 drawn by the short-cut method. (For the cone-of-vision check, see next figure.)

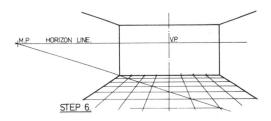

STEP 6.

of the floor and the walls and the ceiling and the walls. At this stage it is necessary to ascertain the limits of the picture, in other words to use the cone of vision.

The cone-of-vision check is shown in Fig.155 and requires that the position of the spectator be known. This is not difficult to locate because, before a perspective drawing of a room can be carried out, there must be a room to draw. This means that its size is known and therefore the distance between the spectator and the picture plane can be established easily. When this measurement is known it is set out on an extension of the centre line of vision. From this point on the centre line of vision a line is set out at 30° to it, to represent half of the 60° cone of vision. The other half of the cone of vision can be located by measurement, as shown in Fig.155, or by repeating the line representing half of the cone of

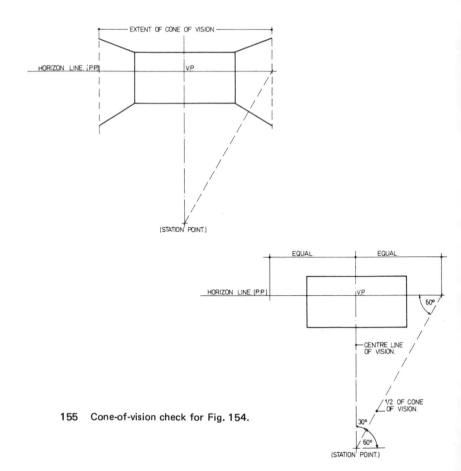

155   Cone-of-vision check for Fig. 154.

vision on the other side of the centre line of vision. When this has been done it is possible to proceed with the construction.

Step 4. A measuring point for the diagonals of square floor tiles was found in Fig. 77 by drawing a sight line parallel to those diagonals and, because the diagonals of the square tiles are at an angle of $45°$ to the picture plane, the distances between the station point and the picture plane and between the vanishing point and the measuring point are the same. (A right-angled isosceles triangle is formed.) This means that the measuring point for the diagonals of square floor tiles will be located at the same distance from the V.P. as the spectator is located from the picture plane. This can be set out on whichever side of the centre line of vision is the more convenient. From this measuring point a line is then drawn through the nearest intersection of the end wall, the side wall and the floor. If the divisions are required on the ceiling, the intersection of the end wall, the side wall and the ceiling is used.

Step 5. Because the end wall of the room is located in the picture plane, the floor tiles can be measured and, using the vanishing point, the longitudinal divisions of the tiles can be drawn as shown.

Step 6. Using the line from the measuring point established in Step 4, the lateral divisions of the square floor tiles are located and drawn, parallel to the end wall.

Once these square floor tiles are located in the room they can be treated as units of measurement and used to locate room features such as doors and windows, furniture and fittings. One can see how easy it would be to locate a door which could be measured in units on the plan of the room, and transferred to the perspective view where it could be drawn in its correct position. Because of the simplicity of this it is not proposed to develop the idea further at this stage, but this principle is used for later examples where it is explained more fully.

Fig. 156 shows the basic or normal one-point perspective construction of a simple cube. Fig. 157 shows the measuring-point method of setting up a simple cube in perspective. If these two figures are compared it will be seen that the results obtained from identical conditions are exactly the same. From the similarity between the interior perspective constructed using the measuring-point method

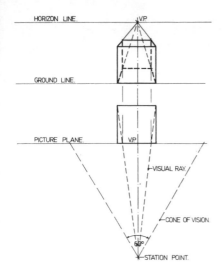

156 A cube in one-point perspective: normal method.

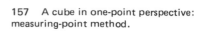

157 A cube in one-point perspective: measuring-point method.

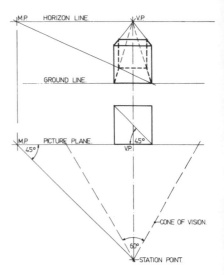

shown in Fig.77 and the one-point construction of the cube shown in Fig.157 it should be obvious that the same basic principle can be used for a short-cut method for setting up a one-point perspective view of a simple cube. The short-cut method, shown in Fig. 158, is as follows:

Step 1. In a convenient position on a sheet of paper draw a horizontal line to represent the horizon line in the perspective view. At a convenient point on this line locate the vanishing point (V.P.) and draw a vertical line through it to represent the centre line of vision.

Step 2. Locate the ground line at the required distance below the horizon line. At this stage it is wise to check with the cone of vision and locate the limits of the picture. This is done by locating a station point, at the required distance from the horizon line (picture plane), on the extended centre line of vision. From this

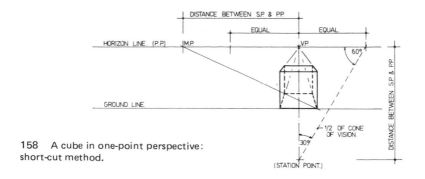

158   A cube in one-point perspective:
short-cut method.

station point a line is drawn at 30° to the centre line of vision
to represent half of the cone of vision; the other half of the cone
of vision is located by measurement. By measurement along the
centre line of vision, as in previous short-cut methods, the
location of the ground line is checked to ensure that it is within
the cone of vision.

Step 3. When the ground line has been confirmed the true elevation
of the cube is drawn. (The front face of the cube coincides with
the picture plane.)

Step 4. A measuring point (vanishing point for the diagonal of a
square) is located on the horizon line at the same distance from
the V.P. as the station point was located from the picture plane
(horizon line).

Step 5. From each of the four corners of the true elevation of the
cube, lines are drawn back to the vanishing point.

Step 6. From the measuring point, a line is drawn to the far base
corner of the true elevation of the cube. At the point where this
line intersects the line from the other base corner back to the
vanishing point will be located the back face of the cube. Using
this, the one-point perspective view of the cube can be completed as shown.

Because the conditions used for this example are exactly the same
as those used for Figs.156 and 157 the result obtained is identical,
which means that this short-cut method is reliable. It also adds
another four possible views to the eight already obtainable by

157

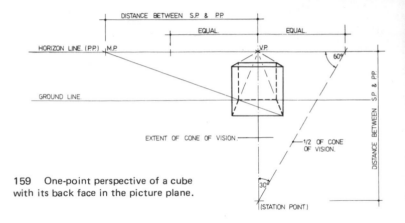

DISTANCE BETWEEN S.P & P.P

EQUAL. EQUAL.

HORIZON LINE. (P.P.) M.P. V.P. 60°

GROUND LINE

DISTANCE BETWEEN S.P. & P.P.

EXTENT OF CONE OF VISION. — 1/2 OF CONE OF VISION.

159   One-point perspective of a cube
with its back face in the picture plane.

30°

(STATION POINT.)

previous short-cut methods, i.e. $45°/45°$ and $60°/30°$, which
further reduces the possibility of not obtaining a satisfactory view
of an object by using short-cut methods. Fig.159 shows the same
short-cut method as used in Fig.158 but in this example the cube
is placed so that its back face coincides with the picture plane.
The only difference between this example and the one immediately preceding it is that the near base corner on the ground line
is used for the line from the measuring point, and the cube is
drawn in front of the ground line instead of behind it.
    Fig.160 shows one use of this principle where a grid of some
required unit can be set out accurately in the perspective view so
that an object can be simply constructed on it. In this example AB
is the required unit and because the grid is to be laid out on the
ground plane the unit measurement AB is set out on the ground

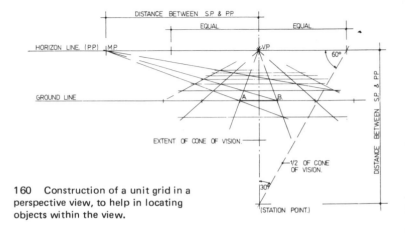

DISTANCE BETWEEN S.P & P.P

EQUAL. EQUAL.

HORIZON LINE. (P.P.) M.P. V.P. 60°

GROUND LINE A. B.

DISTANCE BETWEEN S.P. & P.P.

EXTENT OF CONE OF VISION. — 1/2 OF CONE OF VISION.

30°

160   Construction of a unit grid in a
perspective view, to help in locating
objects within the view.

(STATION POINT.)

line. From this stage forward the construction should be obvious; however, reference to Figs.158 and 159 should clear up any possible confusion.

These short cuts can be of enormous help to the student once he thoroughly understands the principles behind them. Their potential is limited only by lack of imagination, or unwillingness to study and understand the basic principles of perspective projection before using short cuts. The short cuts explained here are by no means all that are available but they form the basis of most, if not all, of the reliable ones and it is from these that others have been and can be evolved. However, to this stage only short-cut methods for setting up the basic shapes of objects have been considered. Others are available for setting up details, shadows etc., which can be used with equal success with either basic perspective constructions or short-cut constructions. The first of these to be considered is the short-cut method for constructing shadows on a perspective drawing.

Fig.161 shows the normal method used for locating the vanishing points for the actual light rays and their plans. (Both V.2 and V.3 are shown but only one, never both, will be required in a drawing.) If Fig.161 is examined (see also Figs. 100-107) it will be seen that the station point, the picture plane and the horizon line are all essential for the construction used to locate the vanishing points for the actual light rays and their plans. In the 45°/45° short-cut method and the 60°/30° short-cut method (see Figs.131 and 135) the horizon line and the picture plane coincide, therefore both are

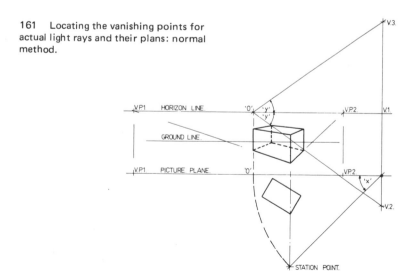

161   Locating the vanishing points for actual light rays and their plans: normal method.

available for use individually in the construction if necessary. The station point was not necessary in the short-cut construction so it was not located but, because it is necessary for the construction to locate the vanishing points for the actual light rays and their plans, it will now be necessary to locate it. This simply consists of drawing a sight line parallel to a side of the object from its vanishing point back to meet the centre line of vision. The station point will be located at the intersection of this sight line and the centre line of vision. Fig.162 shows the station points located on both the 45°/45° and the 60°/30° constructions. Once this is done all of the requirements exist on both short-cut methods for the construction to locate the vanishing points for the actual light rays and their plans.

If the light rays meet the picture plane at angle x and the ground plane at angle y, exactly the same construction as was used in Figs. 101 and 102 is used to locate the required vanishing points. Fig.163 shows the construction superimposed on both the 45°/45° and the 60°/30° to locate the vanishing point for the plans of the light rays (V.1, which is located in the horizon line) and the vanishing point for the actual light rays when the light source is located behind the

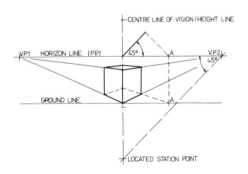

162   Cubes in the 45°/45° and 60°/30° constructions: location of the station point.

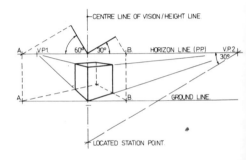

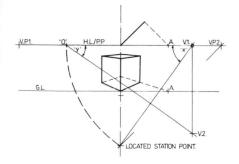

163 Location of the vanishing points for actual light rays (V.1) and their plans (V.2). The light is coming from behind the spectator.

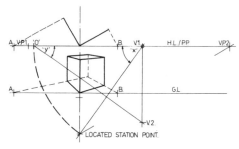

spectator (V.2, which is located below the horizon line). The steps are as follows:

Step 1. From the station point draw a line to meet the picture plane (horizon line/picture plane) at the angle x. The vanishing point (V.1) for the plans of the light rays is located at this intersection. A vertical line is then drawn through V.1 because the vanishing point for the actual light rays, from a light source behind the spectator, will be located directly below V.1

Step 2. Using V.1 as the centre of a circle with a radius equal to the distance between V.1 and the station point, swing an arc to meet the picture plane (horizon line/picture plane) at point O.

Step 3. From point O in the horizon line/picture plane draw a line at the angle y below the horizon line/picture plane to meet the vertical line through V.1 The vanishing point for the actual light rays (V.2.) will be located at this point of intersection.

Fig. 164 shows the construction for the location of the vanishing points for the actual light rays and their plans when the light source is located in front of the spectator. The difference between this

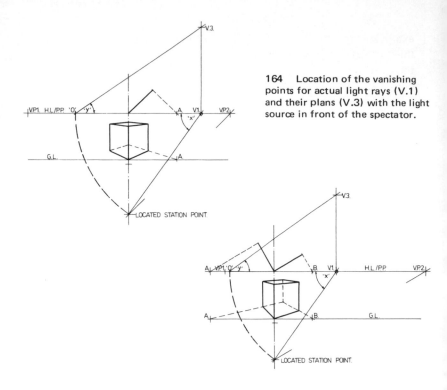

164 Location of the vanishing points for actual light rays (V.1) and their plans (V.3) with the light source in front of the spectator.

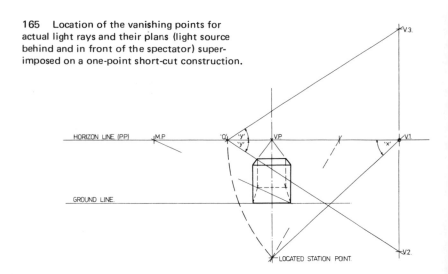

165 Location of the vanishing points for actual light rays and their plans (light source behind and in front of the spectator) super-imposed on a one-point short-cut construction.

example and the ones in Fig.163 is that the angle y is set out above the horizon line/picture plane instead of below it. (V.3 is used when the light source is in front of the spectator.) When the vanishing points for the actual light rays and their plans have been located the shadows are drawn in the normal way (see Figs.103a and 104a).

Because the station point is located in the one-point short-cut method (see Fig.158), it is a simple matter to locate the vanishing points for the actual light rays and their plans. Fig.165 shows the construction for these vanishing points superimposed on the one-point short-cut construction with both V.2 and V.3 located on the one drawing.

This means that even if short-cut methods are employed to set up a perspective view of an object, the correct shadows can still be constructed if necessary. From these constructions used to locate the vanishing points for the actual light rays and their plans it is possible to ascertain factors which are common to all cases:

(1) The vanishing point for the plans of the light rays will always fall in the horizon line.

(2) The vanishing point for the actual light rays will always be either directly below (when the light source is located behind the spectator) or directly above (when the light source is located in front of the spectator) the vanishing point for their plans (V.1).

(3) Angle x (the angle which the plan of a light ray makes with the picture plane) can equal any angle between $0°$ and $360°$ unless a specific direction is given on the plan.

(4) Angle y (the angle which an actual light ray makes with the ground plane) can equal any angle between $0°$ and $90°$ unless a specific angle of inclination is given.

Fig. 166 shows the possible angles for the light source in relation to a plan of an object, a picture plane and a station point. Fig.167 shows the possible angles for the light source in relation to an elevation of an object, a picture plane and a spectator point. Figs. 166 and 167 show that there is a very large number of possible combinations which can be chosen for the location of a light source. This means that if the choice of a light source is left to the student he should be able to select one which is well-suited to his subject. Under these circumstances it is possible to use a short-cut method for locating the vanishing points for the actual light rays and their plans. To explain this, a simple figure is set up using the $60°/30°$ short-cut method (Fig.168). (After the first diagram the perspective construction is omitted to avoid confusion.)

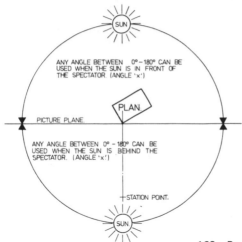

ANY ANGLE BETWEEN 0°–180° CAN BE USED WHEN THE SUN IS IN FRONT OF THE SPECTATOR. (ANGLE 'x')

PLAN.

PICTURE PLANE.

ANY ANGLE BETWEEN 0°–180° CAN BE USED WHEN THE SUN IS BEHIND THE SPECTATOR. (ANGLE 'x')

STATION POINT.

166 Possible angles of direction for a light source — 0° to 360°.

167 Possible angles of inclination for a light source — 0° to 90°.

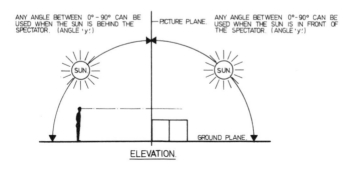

ANY ANGLE BETWEEN 0°–90° CAN BE USED WHEN THE SUN IS BEHIND THE SPECTATOR. (ANGLE 'y')

PICTURE PLANE.

ANY ANGLE BETWEEN 0°–90° CAN BE USED WHEN THE SUN IS IN FRONT OF THE SPECTATOR. (ANGLE 'y')

GROUND PLANE.

ELEVATION.

Step 1. When the direction of the light rays has been decided upon, i.e. whether the light source is to be in front of or behind the spectator and whether it is on his left or his right, one vertical of the object can be chosen as a starting point (*A-A1*). In this example a light source has been chosen behind and to the left of the spectator. From the point where the vertical meets the ground plane (*A*) a line representing a plan of a light ray is

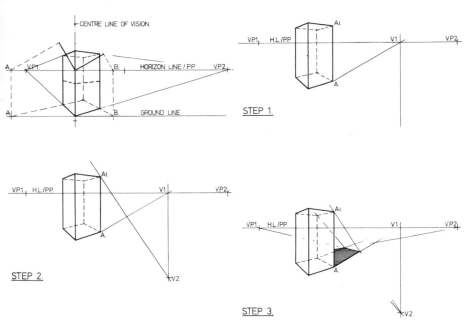

168　60°/30° short-cut construction
with light source behind the spectator.

drawn in the required direction to meet the horizon line/
picture plane, thus locating the vanishing point for the plans
of the light rays (V.1). A vertical line is then drawn through
V.1 (below the horizon line/picture plane in this example,
because the light source is located behind the spectator).

Step 2. Through the top of the vertical line (*A1*) an actual
light ray is drawn at the desired angle and continued to
meet the vertical line drawn through V.1, thus locating the
vanishing point (V.2) for the actual light rays.

Step 3. Once the vanishing points for the actual light rays and
their plans have been located the shadow can be drawn in the
usual way.

Fig. 169 shows an object set up in perspective using the 45°/45°
short-cut method. In this example a light source has been chosen
in front of the spectator and to his right. The vanishing point for the

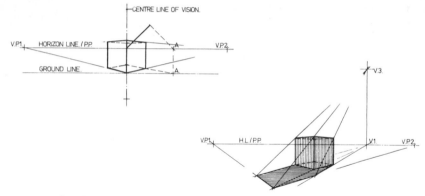

169 45°/45° short-cut construction
with light source in front of the
spectator.

plans of the light rays is located in exactly the same way as it was in
Fig.168. V.3 is located above the horizon line/picture plane by
drawing an actual light ray at the desired angle.

If the results obtained in Figs. 168 and 169 are examined it will
be seen that they both contain the four common factors mentioned
earlier and are therefore the correct results for the chosen sets of
circumstances. In other words, even though the exact angles for
x and y are not known it would be a simple matter to work backwards and find them if this were necessary. This short-cut method
for locating the vanishing points for the actual light rays and their
plans can be used in constructing believable shadows on a perspective
set-up using the basic method. Fig.170 shows a rectangular prism
set up in perspective using the basic method. Once the direction of
the light source has been decided it is a simple matter to select a
vertical as a starting point and to draw from its base, i.e. its intersection with the ground plane, a line representing the plan of a
light ray to meet the horizon line. Through the top of the vertical of the object an actual light ray can be drawn at the desired
angle to meet a vertical line drawn through the vanishing point
for the plans of the light rays (V.1). This intersection will be the
vanishing point for the actual light rays (V.3 in this example,
because the light source decided upon is in front of the spectator;
if it were behind him V.2, which is located below the horizon line,
would be used). When the required vanishing points have been
located, the shadow can be drawn in the normal way.

166

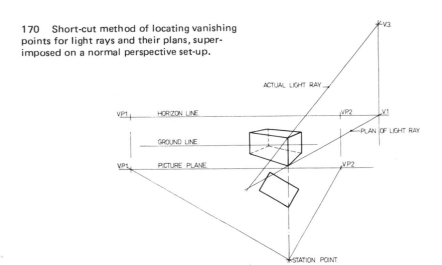

170 Short-cut method of locating vanishing points for light rays and their plans, superimposed on a normal perspective set-up.

Once this short-cut method is understood shadows can be located and drawn so that they are consistent, which is very important, but above all with accuracy and speed. Though, as previously stated, angles *x* and *y* are unknown, the results obtained will be accurate for the set of circumstances chosen arbitrarily. This arbitrary choice of a light source is acceptable in nearly all cases where specific directions are not known. Even if the specific directions are known this method can be used if applied intelligently, i.e. the direction of the travel of the sun would be known, which means that the light source could be placed within these limits and the elevation estimated fairly accurately for that specific position. However, it is not intended to go further into the application of the short-cut method for locating the vanishing points for the actual light rays and their plans. If the theory behind the short-cut method is fully understood the solution of any problem involving the construction of shadows on any type of perspective drawing should be simple.

To this stage, only short cuts for the construction of shadows cast by the sun have been considered. Shadows cast by artificial light sources are considered to be so simple to construct that the basic method, which is very quick and accurate, would be almost impossible to simplify further.

Another short-cut method which will be found to be of considerable use is a further extension of the diagonal theory. So far the diagonal has been used to divide squares and rectangles into equal

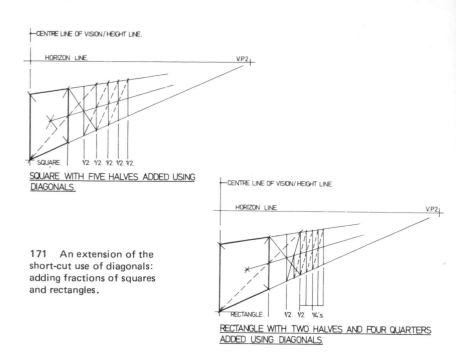

SQUARE WITH FIVE HALVES ADDED USING DIAGONALS.

171 An extension of the short-cut use of diagonals: adding fractions of squares and rectangles.

RECTANGLE WITH TWO HALVES AND FOUR QUARTERS ADDED USING DIAGONALS.

parts or to add further squares or rectangles of equal size to the original one. The diagonal can be used in other ways as well, the obvious ones being the addition of halves or quarters of squares or rectangles, as shown in Fig.171. These are self-explanatory and it will be realized that these additions need not be limited only to halves and quarters of squares or rectangles, but can be used for a variety of additions of various proportions as necessary. The use of the diagonal for dividing squares or rectangles in a perspective drawing into unequal parts or unequal recurring divisions can be a great time-saver.

Fig.172 shows the method used for dividing a rectangular surface into a number of unequal parts using the diagonal. The required divisions are shown on the elevation of the rectangular surface. By drawing a diagonal on this elevation the intersections of this diagonal and the vertical divisions can be projected back to one of the ends of the rectangular surface, where they can be measured. These measurements can then be transferred to the height line in the perspective drawing and perspective lines drawn from each of these measured points to the appropriate vanishing point (V.P.2 in this example). The diagonal is then drawn on the

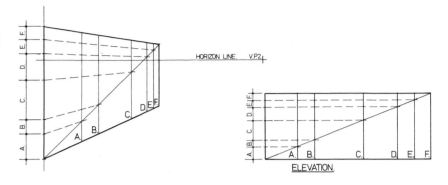

172 Dividing a rectangular surface into unequal
sections by the use of diagonals.

perspective view of the rectangular surface to correspond with the
one drawn on the elevation. The vertical divisions can then be drawn
through the intersections of the diagonal and the perspective lines.
In this example either diagonal could be used because either would
produce the same result; however, it is wise to develop, from the
beginning, the habit of using the diagonal which corresponds to the
one used in the elevation because it can, in many cases, eliminate
confusion.

The possible uses of diagonals in this way, and their variations, are
almost unlimited as they can be used with all of the basic methods
for setting up perspective views of objects, as well as for all of the
short-cut methods. An example of the use of the diagonal in this
way is illustrated in Fig.173, which shows a rectangular face set up

173 A rectangular surface divided into sections,
drawn in perspective by the use of diagonals.

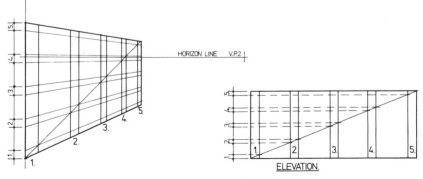

in the perspective view. The elevation in this example shows that the surface is divided into five small spaces of equal size and four large spaces of equal size. The diagonal is drawn on the elevation and the intersections of this diagonal and the vertical divisions are then projected to one of the ends of the rectangular surface where they can be measured. These measurements are then transferred to the height line of the perspective drawing, where perspective lines are drawn on the rectangular surface and the diagonal is drawn to correspond with the one on the elevation. The vertical divisions are located at the intersections of the perspective lines and the diagonal.

One application of this is the breaking-up of a surface of a building which consists of a number of columns with spaces between them. The advantages of the short-cut method in this type of drawing should be obvious. Once the columns and the spaces between them have been drawn in the perspective view it is not uncommon to have to divide the spaces between the columns into a number of further parts representing window mullions, etc.

In the example shown in Fig.174 each space between the columns is required to be divided into four equal parts. The columns have been located using the method shown in Fig.173 but, to avoid confusion, this construction is not shown. To divide the spaces between the columns it is necessary to measure four equal divisions on one of the verticals of the rectangular face. Any vertical may be used but normally the most convenient is chosen and any convenient divisions may be used provided they are equal divisions. Perspective lines are drawn from these divisions as shown and, in this case, because it is only the spaces between the columns which are to be divided, the diagonals are drawn from the intersection of the vertical line repre-

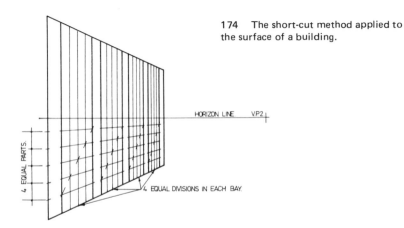

174   The short-cut method applied to the surface of a building.

HORIZON LINE   V.P.2

4 EQUAL PARTS.

4 EQUAL DIVISIONS IN EACH BAY.

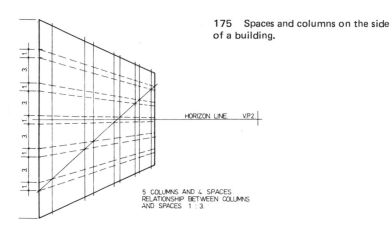

175 Spaces and columns on the side of a building.

HORIZON LINE   V.P.2.

5 COLUMNS AND 4 SPACES
RELATIONSHIP BETWEEN COLUMNS
AND SPACES 1 : 3.

senting a side of the column and the bottom perspective line to the
intersection of the opposite vertical line representing the next column
and the top perspective line. This is repeated in each space between
each pair of columns. The required vertical divisions are then drawn
through the intersections of the perspective lines and the diagonal.
Though four spaces were required in this example, it should be
obvious that any number of spaces could be produced using this
method: it is simply a matter of measuring the required number of
equal spaces on a vertical of the face and proceeding as described.

One variation of this method which can be used for locating the
columns of a building when the ratio between the width of the
columns and the width of the spaces is either known or can be
ascertained is shown in Fig.175. In this example the ratio between
the columns and the spaces is 1 : 3. Using a convenient vertical of
the rectangular face in the perspective drawing and a convenient
scale, set out the required number of measurements in the proportion 1 : 3. These measurements can be set out anywhere on
the vertical and can use either the whole of the vertical or part
of it, as is the case in the example shown here.

From the preceding examples it can be seen that once the
shape of the rectangular face has been located in the perspective
view, irrespective of whether that face has been located using one
of the basic methods of perspective projection or one of the many
short-cut methods, details on that surface, whatever they may be,
can be added using any one of these methods or combinations of
them. Needless to say that although only vertical surfaces have
been shown here the same principles apply to both horizontal

171

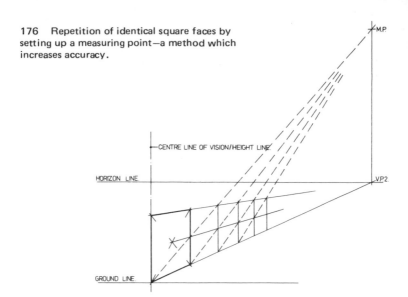

176 Repetition of identical square faces by setting up a measuring point—a method which increases accuracy.

CENTRE LINE OF VISION/HEIGHT LINE

HORIZON LINE

GROUND LINE

M.P.

V.P.2

and inclined planes or surfaces, therefore it is not considered necessary to show them.

Another factor which should be obvious from the preceding examples, particularly Figs.171 and 174, is that the diagonals of equal spaces are parallel, which means that they will converge to common vanishing points (known as measuring points). Though the use of these measuring points is not essential it can be advantageous in so far as it often increases the accuracy of the resulting drawing. Fig.176 shows in perspective a simple square face to which further squares are required to be added. These can be drawn as previously described. However, if the diagonal located by dividing the 'back' edge of the square in halves and drawing a line from the 'front' lower corner of the original square through the centre of the line forming the 'back' edge is continued to meet a vertical line through V.P.2, this intersection will be the vanishing point for this diagonal and all diagonals parallel to it (M.P.). The use of this M.P. will increase the accuracy of the over-all drawing because the location of the vertical lines of the square faces will no longer be the result of a short line located by eye.

The short-cut methods shown here are by no means all that are available for the preparation of a perspective view of an object. They are reliable, as has been shown by relating them back to the already proven basic methods for perspective projection, which means that they can be used confidently without any loss of accuracy. It is undeniable that they are considerable time-savers when compared with the basic methods, and in most cases they also save considerable space. These two factors alone justify their use but, when accuracy is added to them, it means that these short-cut methods are indispensable to the professional renderer and therefore are of enormous value to the student. There are, in use by professional renderers and commercial artists, many variations of the short-cut methods shown here but they are nearly all based on the principles discussed here. Unfortunately there are no short-cut methods which eliminate the learning of the basic principles of perspective projection, and without a sound understanding of these basic principles, short-cut methods — both those shown here and others evolved from them — are of little use to the student; in fact they can be more of a hindrance than a help.

Because accuracy is the most important element in a perspective projection any short-cut method which cannot be proven to produce accurate results is useless and should never be used. Proving the accuracy, or otherwise, of a short cut presupposes a sound knowledge of basic perspective projection. Unfortunately, much that commonly passes for knowledge regarding perspective projection is based on some form of misinformation or half-truth which in many areas bears little resemblance to the facts. In this matter we are no doubt the victims of the prevailing atmosphere in modern-day art attitudes with their roots in Impressionism, in which perspective projection underwent a form of disintegration in favour of other elements. These present-day attitudes, whatever their validity for art, have little or no relevance to the requirements of the renderings of architects, interior designers, industrial designers and all others in the general category of technical illustrators rather than artists. The artist produces a work based on his imagination: the technical illustrator is required to produce a work of fact — which can have artistic merit, depending on the personal skill of the technical illustrator, but its first duty is technical accuracy. If the work is without accuracy its author's honesty and integrity are open to serious question. Against such a charge the only rational defence a designer possesses is his sound basic knowledge of his 'tools of trade' and his ability to use them. The ability to present a pictorial view of the true intent of his design is of paramount importance to him, both as a check for himself and as a true statement to his client and the public of his intentions.

Index